SURRENDER
YOUR
WEAPONS

Writing to Heal

Love + Valley Haggard

SURRENDER YOUR WEAPONS

Writing to Heal

VALLEY HAGGARD

Praise for *Surrender Your Weapons*

"Students, individual writers, and teachers will love this book as it offers examples of brave story telling, brilliant moments of writing advice, and sage reflection on the process....Every writer, every teacher of writing, every human needs this book."

—Dr. Cindy Cunningham, Department Chair of English & Director of Literary Arts at Appomattox Regional Governor's School

"*Surrender Your Weapons* is part memoir, part writing guide and all the vulnerable generous genius healing spirit Valley embodies on the page. She has distilled her fierce generosity as a teacher between the pages.

—Camille Adams, LPC, Psychotherapist

"Part memoir, and part how-to, *Surrender Your Weapons* is like a hug from an encouraging best friend who believes in you wholeheartedly and wants you to live your best, most authentic, most creative life now.

—Anne Soffee, author of *Snake Hips: Belly Dancing & How I Found True Love* and *Nerd Girl Rocks Paradise City*

Surrender Your Weapons

First published in 2018 by
Life in 10 Minutes Press
2707 West Cary Street
Richmond, VA 23220

www.lifein10minutes.com

Distributed by IngramSpark
& Life in 10 Minutes Press

ISBN 978–1–949246–02–5

Printed in the United States of America

First Printing, 2018

Thank You

Claire Lewis and Elizabeth Ferris, my not only insanely talented but also ridiculously beautiful editors. My writing wife and genius witch, Bird Cox. The King and Janitor of Life in 10 Minutes, Tim McCready. Sara Berger, Liza Boisineau, and Cindy Cunningham for deep, insightful reads of early first drafts. The innovative, creative, and meticulous design guru, Llewellyn Hensley. Leah Muhlenfeld for being a website powerhouse and a firecracker. Ward Tefft and all the booksellers at Chop Suey Books for being literary rockstars. Thanks to Ben Krumwiede, our podcast genius, for having a vision for L10 and bringing the voices of our writers to life. Sarah and Mary Kay for accepting my past, predicting my future, and telling it like it is in the present. My beautiful and brilliant friends, mentors, teachers, and sponsors who have carried, loved, nurtured, and held me up along the way. My parents for teaching me and giving me the world. My husband Stan for always knowing he would marry a writer, for marrying me, and for staying married to me. Henry Elijah Sterling Haggard for being the most handsome, brilliant boy who has ever lived and teaching me that boys are human too. My students who, I swear to God, are better writers than me, but let me teach them anyway.

About the Cover Art

Towards the end of what was becoming a desperate hunt for the cover for this book, a dear friend gifted me a Sacred Pause Retreat with artist and minister suzanne l. vinson. suzanne's mission is to help people find sacred beauty through the art of daily living and I did indeed have a nourishing and sacred experience sewing, drawing, and painting in her studio. When suzanne and I decided we'd love to lead art and writing retreats together, she mentioned she'd once illustrated the words "Put Down Your Weapons." Fireworks went off in my head! suzanne's explosive gardens of sacred imagery and color look like a place I want to live. The cover she made for this book illustrates how I feel when I'm at my happiest and most creative. When I've put my weapons down.
— Valley Haggard

I fell in love with Valley's words when reading *The Halfway House for Writers*, and the section entitled "Surrender Your Weapons" caught my breath. Her words and presence reached out from the page and pulled me in. Valley's invitation and her guiding presence have been a healing balm as I practice surrendering my own weapons of self criticism, doubt, and dismissal of my voice. Creating the cover for this book, I held onto her balm and beauty as I aimed to create a reflection of Valley — something of what I see when I look to her — vibrancy, life, radical love — and hiding in plain sight the symbols of her life and writing love story. What a tremendous gift to practice, to play, and to embody healing in the creation of this cover design and co-creation with our guide Valley Haggard.
— suzanne l. vinson

suzanne l. vinson witnesses the sacred as an artist and ordained minister. She gathers folks to the table to make space for wholeness and creativity through her art practice and retreats. Visit suzanne at silvertreeart.com.

Thank you to Wolfgang Jasper for his magic with the camera and the head-shot for this book. Visit Wolfgang at wolfgangjasperphotography.com.

Contents

INTRODUCTION   21

MAY YOU TRUST WHAT COMES   23

FOR HEALING CIRCLES   25

RULES OF SURRENDER   27

CHAPTER 1   Surrender Your Weapons

WHEN OUR WRITING BEGINS   33

A TOOL FOR HEALING   34

SURRENDER TO THE PROCESS   35

OWNING OUR POWER   36

PITY THE FOOL WHO CROSSES A WRITER OF NONFICTION   37

THE ALTAR OF ART   38

LAUGHING RAINBOW   39

CHAPTER 2   Write Your Origin Story

WRITE YOUR ORIGIN STORY   45

ORIGIN STORY   46

MY GRANDMOTHER'S JOURNALS   48

WRITE WHAT HAPPENED   49

PILGRIMS TO MECCA   50

WRITE YOUR MAP   51

CONNECT THE DOTS   52

OLD BONES   56

CHAPTER 3   **Writing the Body**

WRITING THE BODY   61

MOUNTAIN BABY   62

IS THAT ME?   68

THE WAY I FEEL ABOUT MY WRITING
    IS THE WAY I FEEL ABOUT MYSELF   70

CHAPTER 4   **Writing Addiction**

WRITING ADDICTION   75

WRITING SOBER   76

WRITING FOOD   78

HUNGER   79

WRITING MONEY   80

BRONXVILLE THEATRE   82

WRITING SEX   83

SUN GOD   84

EVERYTHING I COULD   85

CHAPTER 5   **Writing Grief**

WRITING GRIEF   88

WAVE   89

WRITING YOUR OWN DEATH   90

WRITING IS SOMETHING WE CAN DO
    WHEN THERE'S NOTHING ELSE THAT CAN BE DONE   91

PROM QUEEN   92

WHAT TO KEEP AND WHAT TO GIVE AWAY   96

THE ART OF THE UGLY CRY   99

CHAPTER 6   **Writing to Heal**

UNZIPPING	105
NEVER GO TO HELL WITHOUT VIRGIL	106
THE FUEL OF FEELING	108
BAD VALLEY	109
WRITE YOUR ALTER EGO	110
WILD THING	111
HOW WE HELP	113
CREATIVE VS. DESTRUCTIVE RISKS	115
THE GREATER THE FEAR	117
HOW TO SURVIVE PUBLIC HUMILIATION	118
ADULT WOMAN	120
SIGNED, SEALED, AND DELIVERED	122

CHAPTER 7   **Writing God**

WRITING RELIGION	129
WRITING MEDITATION	131
DEAR GOD...	132
WRITING PRAYER	133
THE REAL JOURNEYS	134
A CALLING TO WRITE	136
BREATH OF FIRE	137
UPPER WORLD	138
SHIT LIST, WISH LIST, THANK YOU LIST	139

CHAPTER 8   Write the Power

WRITE THE POWER   143

WRITING THE RESISTANCE   144

NAMES OF EXOTIC GODS AND CHILDREN   146

CHOICE   149

WRITING ABOUT RACE   151

WHY I'M NOT BREAKING UP WITH THE WORLD JUST YET   153

WRITING WARRIOR   154

WARRIOR TRAINING   155

CHAPTER 9   After the Ceasefire

CEASEFIRE   159

WHAT DO I WRITE ABOUT NOW?   160

WATER SEEKS ITS OWN LEVEL   162

GET BORING, GIRL   164

YOU ARE WRONG   165

GO AWAY   167

WRITING THE COPY   168

OVER OUR HEADS   169

VULTURES TO CARRION   171

TAKE IT ALL OUT   172

STITCH YOUR STORY TOGETHER   174

THE NON-WRITING WRITER   175

CHAPTER 10 **Miraculous Birth**

BIRTHS AND BOOKS   179

CRAFT   180

LIBRARIES INSIDE ME   181

OOPS! I ACCIDENTALLY SELF-PUBLISHED MY FIRST BOOK   182

WRITING BABY   184

WRITING EVERYONE CAN UNDERSTAND   186

THE PEOPLE WHO WRITE WITH ME   188

MIRACULOUS BIRTH   189

MINE   193

Introduction

Surrender Your Weapons. We have abused and belittled ourselves long enough. We have been our own worst enemies, our own worst critics, the harshest arbiters on Judgment Day. We have ignored and neglected our writing altogether or shot it down in infant form, before it had a chance to take its first breath. The first rule of the Halfway House is to stop, to arrest our masochistic tendencies, and let our work be what it is.

— *The Halfway House for Writers*

Surrender Your Weapons is the first rule of the Halfway House. Of all the lessons I've needed to learn as a writer and a human being, this is the one that resurfaces most. Weapons take many forms and manifestations, most of which we seem to wield against ourselves. Judgment, comparison, impossible expectations, perfectionism, doubt, insecurity, destructive behavior, self-sabotage. My Surrender Your Weapons workshop drops us straight into the heart of our material in a safe environment where we don't judge ourselves or others. It's here that our true writing and our true selves begin to emerge.

Surrender Your Weapons is a marriage of selections from my memoir, *Miraculous Birth,* and a writing guide for healing, exploring themes that have emerged in my classes and in my own writing since the publication of *The Halfway House for Writers* in 2015.

Surrender Your Weapons is intended to be a guide for writing your story while showing you how I wrote mine. I hope that for you, like for me, healing happens along the way.

May You Trust What Comes

May you bring forth what is within you
May you walk through the fire of your stories
May you swim through the ocean of your words
May you dive bravely into the water of your memories
May you build the house of your body
May you write the story of your life
May you tell the stories that gut you, that heal you
May you surrender to the process
May you trust what comes
May you go deeper into your life, into the truth,
than you've ever gone before
May you surface from the wreckage with rubies
and stories and emeralds and gold
May you let sand and salt scrub you clean
May you follow your own thread through to the end
May you be your own heroine, hero, warrior, and muse
May you surrender your weapons
May you trust what comes

For Healing Circles

We find each other. We who have been harmed by good intention. We who have been harmed by touch. We who have been harmed by abusive language. We who have been prey to those who seek to do us harm. We bind ourselves to one another in a spirit of healing. Our spoken and unspoken stories go into a sacred trust. Through our sharing and caring we create healing circles of growing support.

—suzanne l. vinson, *Broken Wide Whole: Prayers for Daily Living*

The Rules of Surrender

1. Surrender Your Weapons

Whether our battles have been within ourselves or out in the world, when we come to the page it's time to surrender our weapons. It's time to be who we are beneath our armor so we can show up in our writing in a way that is honest and vulnerable and true. If our fortress has been invaded by criticism or self-doubt, comparison or apology, self-sabotage or judgment, we must seek shelter and create safety. We must surrender our weapons so we can pick up the tools necessary to create and to begin.

2. Right Now I Am

When you sit down to write, start with the words "Right Now I Am." Starting in the present moment helps ground us in our bodies and on the page. It helps us get centered, get current, arrive. Writing down what's on our minds, without judgment or censorship, washes away the debris keeping us stuck and allows us to move into the deeper layers buried beneath the fragments of the day.

We might have to wade for miles through the muck before we find an ounce of treasure. We might have to write incoherently or haltingly or messily before we find our voice or hit our stride. We might have to write out grocery lists and to-do lists, song lyrics or news reports, commercials, jingles, or fragments of dreams. We might have to toss away a lot of trash before we strike gold. "Right Now I Am" is our imperial and holy dumping ground. It connects us to everything we need to find or discover.

Start where you are right now. You can trust that you are headed in the right direction if you are writing at all.

3. Extract Your Splinters

I think of writing practice as a process of extracting splinters. Whether you extract the biggest splinter or the smallest first doesn't matter. You may choose the shard piercing your foot or the thorn in your side. Just keep going. Keep extracting splinters, one at a time. Each time I sit down to write, I start with an internal mental, emotional, spiritual, and physical body scan, seeking out sore spots that, left to fester, will become infected. Wherever there is a splinter still lodged—age old or brand new—I extract it by naming it, by writing it out until it has lost some of its sting, some of its power. Only then can I move on. The pen is the tweezers, the lance, and the sword. It is the surgeon's knife with the power to cut and ultimately, to heal.

4. Push Gently Against Your Comfort Zone

Feel out the walls of your comfort zone and then give a gentle push. Facing our fears adds fire and fuel to our writing. It helps us expand, grow, and take creative risks. We do not want to keep our writing constricted and small. We do not want to shrink to take up less space, but we also don't have to go further or faster than we are ready to go. We can go at our own pace, in our own time. Push gently against your comfort zone. See how expansive and big and brave your writing wants to become.

5. Handwrite. Freewrite. Listen.

Handwrite. Writing by hand is a basic, primal practice that creates a direct connection between our heads, hearts, and hands. Writing by hand sets a pace that encourages the hectic thoughts in our heads to slow down, filtering out excess words and thoughts, allowing us to hone in on what matters most.

Freewrite. Freewriting gives us a place to wander, play, explore, process, and be. It's a safe place to set aside perfectionism, finished drafts, left brain logistics, and the compulsion to get everything right.

Listen. Listen to your own stories and the stories of others. Listening connects us to each other, creates community, transforms the personal into the universal, and shows us the surprising ways in which we relate to each other. When we listen to others, we collect prompts for ourselves and find our place in the world of story.

When we read our own work out loud we are able to experience what we have written in a new way. When we listen, we process our own words and experiences differently. The body's physical response — laughing, crying, sweating, and shaking — happens most often when we hear our work read aloud. We are able to have compassion for who we are and what we have survived in a whole new way.

6. Cook with Heat

Writing with a timer or another form of structure helps us cook with heat. Timers, writing classes, deadlines, and accountability partners transform our writing from raw ingredients into dishes ready to serve up hot. I have found that ten minutes is long enough to dive deep and resurface without fear of drowning or losing all of our breath. Set the timer for three or ten or twenty minutes to transform your words from tepid to steaming. Experiment and see what works for you.

7. Trust What Comes

Do not turn away the visitors at your door. They come bearing gifts, even those that make you want to slam the door and run.

When we write, we have a tendency to dismiss what comes. We brush off the thought or image or word surfacing in our minds as embarrassing or trivial, shameful or dumb. Instead, invite the word or image flashing through your mind to come in. A fragment, a flash, a shadow, a phrase, no matter how small, has something to reveal. Give it a chance. See where it leads. Trust what comes.

CHAPTER I

Surrender Your Weapons

WHEN OUR WRITING BEGINS

After my mother saw me swinging a chain on the playground to protect myself from the kids who threatened to beat me upside the head, she moved me to another elementary school across town. I carried a bear-handled knife traveling with my girlfriend across Eastern Europe alone. I've scratched, bitten, and hit when I thought I had to. But my best defense has always been my tongue. Sharp, cutting, and deadly words that know where to strike.

For several years I was involved in an online sado-masochistic affair. Words were the currency of our weapons and whips. The only way I could begin to repair the psychic damage done was to step out of the ring altogether. I could no longer win or lose. I had to surrender.

I quit drinking, doing drugs, and smoking. Addiction was a war I couldn't win. I had to surrender.

I've berated myself as a writer, let the inner critic dictate subject, pace, tempo, line, and language. The inner critic who said I'd never be a real writer, never be good enough, would never measure up. That was a war I couldn't win. I had to surrender.

When we come to the page it is best we lay down the weapons we hold against ourselves. Shame, secrecy, perfectionism, the violence of self-loathing. Each of these will kill our creativity, damage our self-worth, violate the truth of who we are. Maybe not all at once, but eventually. Slow death by a thousand cuts.

We each have our own power, beauty, strength, and vulnerability to own. We can arrive on the page of our stories without apology, without allowing anyone, including ourselves, to hold us down.

When we surrender to the page, to the process, to the great world of the heart and the spirit that writing inhabits, this is when our writing is able to begin.

We don't have to fight what comes. We just have to let it.

A TOOL FOR HEALING

I am a recovering alcoholic, druggie, smoker, and love addict. I'm a co-dependent emotional eater who has struggled to manage money. I'm a perfectionist with low self-esteem and impossibly high standards. I've had tumors, diseases, surgeries, and miscarriages. Several of my body parts have been sent to pathology. I have experienced loss, grief, heartbreak, anxiety, depression, existential angst, and the dark night of the soul. I've hated God and I've been sure God hated me. Healing, for me, is a mental, emotional, physical, and spiritual full-time job. One I'll never really be able to quit.

I have tried and used 12-step recovery meetings, therapy, prayer, meditation, yoga, Rohun, past life regression, hypnosis, EMDR, mandalas, A Course in Miracles, church, synagogue, satsong, acupuncture, reiki, goddess dance, and witchcraft to try to heal my original and ancient wounds.

All of these have helped and a few have even stuck, but the most consistent healing force in my life has been writing. Expressive writing. Free writing. Journaling. Keeping a diary. Whatever you want to call it. Writing has saved my life.

Much has been written about the research-based positive healing impact writing has on the immune system, as well as the mental, emotional, and physical health of the writer. I'm thrilled scientists have evidence and numbers, but anyone who has used writing in their life consistently already knows. Writing heals.

Of course, I have fought the writing process, too. Hard. To avoid writing I've taken up professional scrap booking, stained glass making, basket weaving, crochet, addictions, bad jobs, and lots of bad habits.

And still, writing has been the healing modality of my life that I've returned to again and again. Writing can be a weapon if we use it against ourselves, but it is also a powerful medicine, an antidote to whatever our poison may be.

SURRENDER TO THE PROCESS

If you'd rather approach writing like a journey through uncharted territory than a trip to the grocery store, it's best to surrender to the creative process. Surrendering to the process means we often don't end up writing what we sat down to write. It means being willing to begin without knowing what's coming next or where we're going to end up. Surrendering to the process means trusting what comes. Even if it initially seems trivial or unimportant, embarrassing or wrong, trust it. The image or thought floating up from your subconscious is the next clue in the mystery of the unknown work you are creating. Follow it.

Some people outline their work knowing exactly what they need to accomplish between points A and B. This method works beautifully for certain types of writers or in specific instances of the writing process. It is a goal-oriented method that achieves quantifiable results. However, I believe if you don't discover something new in your own writing process, your reader won't either.

Letting go of control of our words and stories can feel scary. We might encounter monsters, shadows, humiliations, and memories reaching out from the dark. But these are the elements that create our best stories. And they don't go away if we shove them back down or ignore them, either. They just find a different way to come back into our lives beyond the paper and the pen.

When you surrender to the process, you stop walking into the wind and let it usher you forward. You harness the strength and power of what's been building up inside of you rather than fighting it down.

OWNING OUR POWER

I have poured hours, months, years into obsessions instead of writing or making art.

I've had a habit of obsessing over writers/artists/musicians when the ultimate truth was I didn't want to possess them. I wanted to be them. I have confused my reaction to someone else's creativity or genius as a way to downplay or ignore my own. I've chosen men to worship not because they supported my writing but because they criticized it, confirming what I knew deep down to be true. They were the real deal while I was just a girl, just a mom, a pretender and a fake. Too local, too simple, not good enough, not good enough to take myself seriously.

It's taken a lot of healing, a lot of writing, and a lot of time with people who don't need to tear me down to feel better about themselves to no longer believe that those insults were true.

As creative people with no concrete scale for measuring success, it's too easy to believe that everyone else is a better writer, has crazier stories, deeper truths, more legitimate lives. If we have been marginalized in any way, it takes an incredible amount of strength and stamina just to crawl our way back up to the bottom floor.

The truth is we don't need to judge ourselves from anyone else's vantage point. We have our own castles, our own cliffs, our own mountain peaks, and our own rooftops from which we can soar. Even if it means starting in the basement and searching in the dark for the stairs.

What power and time and resources have you given away? What parts of yourself and your story do you need to reclaim?

36

PITY THE FOOL WHO CROSSES A WRITER OF NONFICTION

At one point, much of my writing was fueled by the desire for revenge. I had to prove how good I really was to those I felt had hurt, betrayed, or belittled me. Who hadn't believed in me, had wronged me. Writing about my life and theirs would be the greatest payback. I would right the emotional wrongs and create justice once and for all.

I would strip them, expose them, and make them finally see.

Pity the fool who crosses a writer of nonfiction, I liked to say, knowing the weapon I had at my disposal.

I needed to write out every word. Not necessarily for them, but for me.

These days, miraculously, after writing so much out and through, I less often feel the need to humiliate my enemies. I have had to write character assassinations, sob stories, yes. But I have not had to publish all of these pieces in a public, flashy way.

At this moment, I don't feel the need to prove my worth by undermining yours.

Telling my story, writing my emotions from my point of view is another thing altogether. That, I have to do.

Whether or not we publish true stories about real people in our lives is a complex, nuanced decision that every nonfiction writer must make for themselves. We must weigh our options and come to our own conclusions.

Some of my published pieces have been painful for other people to read, but I believe writing and sharing them was important for our relationship to heal.

In other cases, the healing began to happen as soon as the words were released onto the page with no need to show them to anyone else at all.

THE ALTAR OF ART

For decades, I was convinced I would sacrifice anything at the Altar of Art. My family, my relationships, my health, and certainly my identity — I wanted a new one anyway. To me, making art out of telling the truth was the top priority, the ultimate goal.

I don't feel this way anymore. At least, I have found it possible to make art that is true without making art that destroys. I have many relationships now that are more sacred to me than anything I could write about them. I would never want to publish anything about my son that would cause him embarrassment or pain. My husband has given me carte blanche to write whatever it is I need to write. In fact, he's said, "Don't leave a word out." But there are some places too sensitive, too sacred to go. In these instances, being a human being is far more valuable to me than being a writer.

This isn't to say I can't write the truth in any and every form I need to: front, back, and underbelly. But what I choose to publish, to put out there into the world, is another story altogether, one I've chosen to be thoughtful and careful in the telling.

A few months ago I wrote a piece I wanted to publish that I knew would be painful for my dad. I meditated, prayed, and sought counsel. My trusted spiritual advisor suggested I send it to him that afternoon, letting him know I wanted to publish it the next day. It was terrifying to show the truths I had written to my dad, but liberating, too. It opened the door for conversation and healing we hadn't had before. It was a risk I'm glad I took.

There are other pieces that live in my notebook and in my notebook alone. While I needed to write them to exorcise them from inside of me, to process, and to heal, they do not need to find their way into the outside world. I know writers who have been disowned by their families because of the personal stories they have written. Some have said good riddance, others have had to work painfully for years to win back trust in a relationship that was destroyed.

I wish there was a checklist or set of guidelines that would help you identify what could ruin your life and what could save it. But there isn't. We each have to make this call, take this risk, find this discernment on our own.

LAUGHING RAINBOW

I win the Good Citizenship Award in first grade. I am very, very nice. I am nice to everybody except my best friend Sarah who is half-Dominican and half-white, has frizzy flyaway hair, and wipes her nose on her sleeve.

When the teacher leaves the room, she leaves me in charge of the class and I am instructed to write the name of anyone who talks on the chalkboard. I write Sarah's name in big print letters even though she hasn't said a word. She's the only kid I know who doesn't want to beat me up. Her mother teaches us Spanish at her house in the afternoons. We invent games like "Mouse in the Computer" and "Fresh Out of College" with her big sister, Paz. We jump out of her loft onto the couch below like we are flying out of this world and into the next.

When the teacher gets back, she makes Sarah write "I will not talk in class when the teacher is away" 100 times. I get the Good Citizenship Award, but I know the truth about me. I am bad to the bone.

Rasheedah says she is going to beat me upside the head if I wear the same shirt again tomorrow. I lean back into the cold, dark brick of the school. I'm wearing peach corduroy bell bottoms with a big sash and a white shirt with a rainbow across the belly, thick strips of red, yellow, orange, green, and blue from the thrift store. I have mousy straight brown hair and green eyes. Rasheedah tells me she is going to slap me upside the head because of my shirt and because I started slavery.

I hold my lunch box like a wedge between my back and the wall, a wedge that will hold me up. The basement of our school is haunted by the ghost of a slave girl. Everyone says. I feel terrible about everything, the dead girl and starting slavery, but mostly I'm afraid of Rasheedah.

Regina lets me sit with her in the cafeteria. They call her Regina Vagina. Rasheedah smacks her lips at us and I cringe and Regina gives me one of her Ho Hos. I am one of a few white kids at the school and the only kid that's Jewish. I feel terrible about wearing my thrift store clothes every day, about having tofu in my lunch. About being left in charge of the class.

I hide my carob tofu celery raisin balls under the lid of my lunch box and rip open the plastic casing of the Ho Ho, fakey fluffy chocolate cake with white sugar goo. I am safe inside the Ho Ho. I hate my mother for not packing them for me herself, these compact confections of love.

I beg my mom to let me stay longer at Sarah's or to have Sarah come to our house. She never mentions the punishment I've made her endure. We play and play and play, like our lives depend on it.

John Hunter is the SPACE teacher at my elementary school, the class for the bright kids. He has a kinky black beard with little mountain peaks spiraling down from his chin beneath smooth flashes of white, a rainbow knit hat atop his giant afro. He listens to everything I say. My thoughts are important to him. He creates circles out of children in the dark, haunted basement that smells like old food and older ghosts. He turns the school into a fortress, a safe cave, the only soft place to fall and to laugh. He holds a ceremony where he renames us, gives us new identities, something for us to both wear and carry, to live in and up to.

He names me Laughing Rainbow. When I'm Laughing Rainbow I inhabit the stories that come out of his mouth, the basement is enchanted and I am safe.

When my mom sees me swinging a chain on the playground to keep the other kids away, she transfers me to the school in our district, less than a mile from our home. In fourth grade I'm the only black-haired Jewish girl in an ocean of blonde pigtails and crew cuts and Republicans and polo shirts. I'm the only kid who doesn't vote for Ronald Reagan in the mock election. Even though I'm closer to home, I feel even more out of place. I miss John Hunter. I miss Sarah. I miss Laughing Rainbow. I've gone from strange to stranger. I don't know how to make friends here or what expression to hold on my face. I have crushes on popular, standoffish rich boys who don't even know my name.

CHAPTER 2

Write Your Origin Story

WRITE YOUR ORIGIN STORY

We all have our own personal mythologies, fairy tales, origin stories. From our parents to our ancestors, known or lost, available or mysterious, living or dead, the people and tribes and cultures we come from create the backstory for who we are today.

I come from Wilhelmina Bjornson and Raymond Smith, Boris and Margaret Yanpolski. I come from Copenhagen, Denmark, and the Pale between Poland and Russia. My people are Jewish, Native American, Eastern European. I come from bureaucrats and anarchists, artists and nurses, academics and country people who worked the land. I come from alcoholism, mental illness, survival, recovery, art, and hard work. My mother is a short, dark-haired beauty and an artist. My father is a tall, handsome carpenter. They are both in recovery. They met at a poetry reading, and during their brief marriage they created me.

A writing teacher once asked me to write my life as if it were a fairytale. I loved seeing my family as royalty; kings, queens, and villains. The archetypal characters who create the story of my life.

Where do you come from? Who are your people? What is the fairytale of your life? I have students who were adopted, who have adopted children of their own, who have disinherited their families for good. Some of us want to find our people and some of us want to get as far away as we possibly can.

Are you the Prodigal Daughter? Who are your Adam and Eve? Your Zeus and Hera? Your Mother Earth and Father Sky? What elements were present in the creation of you?

When we write, we create a legacy whether we choose to hand it down to those who come after us or not.

Tell your origin story. Trace your life back to the beginning of you.

ORIGIN STORY

My mother smoked throughout her pregnancy with me. I grabbed onto her long black locks while she smoked and I breastfed, one of her hands holding onto me, the other at her lips. My mom quit smoking when she saw a commercial with a mother and daughter on our black and white tube TV. "Do you want to live to see her grow up?" the narrator asked. She did. It was 1977. I was two. It was the year her mother died and my dad moved out. I'd already eaten a cigarette. I knew the difference between a Camel and a joint and I'd inserted a peanut in the place I'd seen her put a tampon. I walked around the house naked in cowgirl boots that came up to the tops of my fat, buttery thighs.

But it wasn't my mother I wanted to be when I grew up. I wanted to grow up and get married three times and divorced twice, just like my dad. I wanted to smell like unscented pink ChapStick from the twisty black tube and fresh sawdust and cigarette smoke. I wanted to move at the end of each year into a new apartment or townhouse or rental with a new husband or wife or girlfriend or lover. I wanted to marry my dad but more than that, I wanted to grow up to be just like him, wild and free and never in the same place, doing the same thing, past its expiration, too long.

After I moved out of the house I'd lived in with my mother my entire life except for the one time she moved — across the street — I slept in hostels and motels and tents. I slept in cabins and yurts and the beds of strangers. I slept in dorm rooms and train cars and bus seats and truck beds. I slept in hunting lodges and cruise ships and trailer parks. I slept in as many places, with as many people, as I could.

My dad's second wife wanted me to call her Mommy but I called her Baby instead. I called my dad Snorky and he called me Little Pig. We spoke to each other in high-pitched nasal voices and invented worlds inhabited by talking animals and magical creatures and friendly monsters that did whatever you said. Turn all the house lights on. Turn the music up. Let the faucet run until the house floods into oceans. My mother told me she was concerned that I couldn't tell the difference between reality and make-believe. I like the make-believe world better, I said.

Not sure where they'd gone, I remember pacing the narrow wooden hallways of my dad and Baby's Fan apartment frightened of monsters and robbers and things I didn't know how to name. My mom stopped letting me spend the night at their house and I hated her for that. I wanted as much of my dad as I could get.

When their marriage ended, my dad ended up in rehab. I was crushed not to spend Easter with him that year. My mom was Jewish, did not eat sugar, and made terrible health food Easter baskets. Even though I'd grown up in the back of AA meetings I didn't understand drinking, the allure or meaning of getting drunk. At least not yet.

When I was seven, in the checkout line at Safeway, I asked my dad to marry me. "We should wait until we're 100 though," I told him. I thought that by then my age would have caught up with his.

When I was 22, my fiancé and I moved to Arkansas to live in a tool shed on his father's farm. Our bed was wedged between nests of rakes and shovels and farm equipment while his father slept alone in a tiny cabin he built himself. After a couple of months of waiting tables and smoking weed and drinking everything I could from Ruby's Liquor Store across the dry county line, I decided I was in love with my fiancé's father, the same age as my own. The morning after I moved into Will Senior's king-sized bed, I woke up from a dream screaming, snakes crawling out of my mouth and all around my head.

My dad married for the third and final time when I was twelve. He and my new stepmother have lived in the same house out in the country for the last twenty-five years. They are still in love. Their home and their land in their hard-won life is open and full of air and light and love.

And that love exists inside me too, lit like a lantern in the blackest night. The ripping apart and the merging together, the coming and the going, the leaving and the staying, finally the staying. The many selves I've tried on, wanted to be, the lives I've thought I should live, the converging and twisting and dying and being born again and again, trying to reconcile who I should be, who I really am, and how I want to live.

MY GRANDMOTHER'S JOURNALS

My grandmother's sister was in the playhouse when it caught fire and burned down. My grandmother's mother was never the same after her oldest daughter died. She dressed my grandmother up in her dead sister's clothes every year on the anniversary of the girl's tragic death.

When I was little, my grandma was the perfect grandma to me. I got to visit her and grandpa in their farmhouse in the Blue Ridge Mountains where they raised my father and their five other kids. I was one of dozens of grandchildren yet somehow she made each of us feel important, loved, and special. She taught me how to fold hospital corner sheets when at home I didn't even make my bed. She took me to get my ratty hair permed, bought me a matching blue and white polka dot skirt set to replace my stained thrift store bell bottoms. She talked to me about Jesus, and, as her only Jewish granddaughter, fortified me with a series of Jews for Jesus action adventure romance novels that I devoured in those idyllic weeks of summer I spent at her house in the country.

I didn't learn until I was an adult how much time my grandma spent in and out of mental institutions. I didn't know about her depression, anxiety, shock treatments, about the pain on the inside of a life that looked so perfect on the outside. I just knew that after the service in the chapel of Our Lady of Lourdes convalescent home, she confessed to me she'd never in her life felt good enough to replace the sister she had lost. She was not good enough for anyone, she told me, not even God. I begged my grandma to believe Jesus loved her at least as much as she loved me. I can only hope that some part of her did.

After her death, my father shared my grandmother's journals with me. There must have been thousands of pages in her dear, familiar scrawl describing her joys and her torments, her worries, her deep self-doubt and her abiding love of God. After I read as much as I could, I had a deeper understanding, a more complex, 3D, human view of the woman I had loved so much, but in her life had only partially known.

WRITE WHAT HAPPENED

When we write alone in our journals or diaries we often use a shorthand to vent our feelings rather than describing what happened. Sometimes we need to write to process, to unload, to rant. But it's important that we tell the story of what happened, too. The plot, setting, and characters, what he or she said, are the elements that make a story stand up. What happened is the framework of the house we are trying to build.

David Sedaris's recently published diaries, *Theft by Finding*, contain very few mentions of how he feels, but the reader, when shown what he's overheard, observed, or done, is given the direct sensation of the feelings themselves. When we read what happened we are able to experience the emotions first-hand, rather than through translation. Likewise, when we write theory or philosophy we can get so far adrift in elusive academic language that we lose track of the humanity within the story. Give us the personal details that connect your theory to you. Rather than writing a treatise on love, show us what she did to make you feel it.

Write what happened is another way of saying show, don't tell. Instead of saying "I felt sad," take us with you to the vet where you have to make the terrible decision whether or not to put down your beloved dog. Rather than saying you're angry, describe how your roommate finished your half-and-half and then left crusted dirty dishes piled up in the sink. What was the expression on your mother's face the night your father left?

At times, we all need to write out our interior monologues, hopes, wishes, and feelings in nonlinear, incoherent ways. But it's the solid images, the specific details, the lines of dialogue, and twists of plot that invite the reader to come in and experience life with us, rather than hearing about it.

PILGRIMS TO MECCA

Armed with BB guns and 40 ounces of Schlitz Malt Liquor we exploded windows out of abandoned buildings on Broad Street, sent enormous rats scurrying through the mountains of debris and rubble at our feet. We slept on the train trestles huddled against the cement landing, shivering into each other's warmth as trains rocketed by hundreds of feet above the river. We bought beer and wine and liquor from corner stores and older brothers, piled into each other's second-hand cars, turned the music up and toured the streets of our city like rock stars in a tour bus. We broke into each other's pools and skinny dipped at night in the river, set up camp in the old pump house and picnicked in the lushest gardens of the most beautiful parks. We dyed and cut our own hair, taught each other how to drive and to drink, snuck out of our houses and into each other's bedrooms. We haunted dive bars and all-night diners and apartments of punk bands that were papered with graffiti. We shared each other's boyfriends and girlfriends and lipsticks and leather coats and vintage velvet gowns. We gave each other nicknames and bruises and kisses. We talked philosophy and art and music and literature. We were brilliant and crazy and stupid and wise, sneaking around the law and the man and our own mothers. We wrote poems and letters and ranted and fought and sang and fucked and slept in piles like newborn baby kittens. We betrayed each other and wrote vows to each other and felt our hearts leave and reclaim our bodies for each other. We dropped out of high school and went to college. We went to Outward Bound and to work and other countries. We didn't know that some of us would get wet brain or have liver failure, that we'd die in a house fire or of a heroin overdose, that we'd marry and divorce and move into our childhood homes, becoming husbands and wives and musicians, artists and writers, archaeologists, social workers, mattress salesmen, lawyers, medical librarians, teachers and professors. We didn't know we'd become mothers and fathers with children of our own, that we'd find God and happiness and other cities full of brand new people. But we did know, we always knew, that we'd return eventually like pilgrims to Mecca, our holy stories the creation stories that we told about each other.

WRITE YOUR MAP

Our lives are formed by all kinds of maps. We can follow the trails of cities we have lived in, schools we have attended, jobs we have worked, meals we have eaten, people we have loved. We can follow the map that would be made if we traced our footsteps around the world or our own city.

Sometimes I think of writing memoir, essay, or narrative nonfiction as assembling clues to recreate the mystery novels of our lives. What happened to make us who we are today? What crimes have been committed by or against us? Where did it all happen and who were the key players?

In my teen workshop, Write Your Heart Out, I ask the students to create a recipe for their own hearts. How much of this, how much of that? What ingredients have come together to make us who we are?

I believe not only our physical selves have maps but also our emotional and spiritual selves. Where has our journey taken us? What did we take with us, or leave behind? When I was traveling by Eurorail through Eastern Europe, my girlfriend and I believed if we traced our path on the map we would recreate God's face. The zigzag of my dad's map through the zip codes of our city in all the different places he lived while I was growing up tells an incredible story of moving, leaving, and searching for home. Sometimes our stories take the shape of a narrative, sometimes a list or a prayer.

The ingredients of our hearts can most certainly create poems. The mystery novels of our lives try to make sense of the disparate parts of our selves. Writing our map draws a line from point A to B to C to Z, showing us how we got from there to here, where we are now.

CONNECT THE DOTS

Sometimes I want to start our story of traveling across Eastern Europe on my junior year abroad with the man masturbating into the train window while we had our layover in Basel, Switzerland. Or I could begin with the man masturbating into the Arno in October and end with the man masturbating behind me on the tram in Vienna. Or with the short blond man in the discoteca who takes off his tie and tries to whip me with it while African lesbians dance the Macarena in a line. But that would just be playing connect the dots. Too easy.

When we are on Eurorail we trace our steps across the map. We are sure if we get the lines just right, we will draw the face of God.

I carry my knife with the bear-head handle. She is a double black belt in karate.

In the hostel in Prague a man kicks our door in screaming, "American bitches!"

In Budapest we are scrubbed down naked in the salt baths and then we drink bad beer all night in the hostel bar and since it is open 24 hours we never, ever want to leave.

We see *Jesus Christ Superstar* in Czechoslovakian and she buys the CD, memorizes all the songs, tells me that she is Mary Magdalene.

We are in love in Pompeii and I sing "I Married Isis on the Fifth Day of May" among the ruins. We eat lemon ICEEs before we get back on the tram.

We see *The Little Mermaid* on Christmas Day in Copenhagen, my underwear a ball in my pocket and I think about how she cut out her tongue for legs and still the prince didn't love her.

The Viennese boys choir is beautiful but I am homesick for a home I don't yet have.

All of our drawings crash off the walls at night while we are sleeping.

"I love you more," she says as I leave for the airport.

We are the Little Mermaid. We lose our voices to each other.

I cut off my hair and throw it in the sea.

She bleaches the kitchen wall, behind the stove, leaving a test strip to prove that it really was filthy, that her cleaning was not in vain. She hammers the door in my room so that it will close correctly, so the cold won't seep in, so we won't have to stuff my dresses in the cracks. Splinters fly past her head. She steps on and breaks her Walkman. She accidentally kicks me. She asks for a new God.

This is about me. Gene, our expat art teacher, says that the problem with the twentieth century is that everyone wants to express their individuality and the problem with opinions is that everybody's got one. But this — this is about me.

On the streets, they wear yellow gloves and yell. They honk horns and carry shovels. One pretends to pick another one up by the hair and then they commence honking, digging, demolishing. With all of the continuous construction, I wonder how this city still stands up. Things: blocks of cement, walls, bricks, chunks fall under the feet of the men on the scaffolds. It seems like everything is held together by one tack and no one knows where it is.

I always cry when chopping onions for our dinner. Someone told me it helps to stick an onion on your head and chew Wonder Bread. Instead, I lean in closer to intensify the burn. Tears form, roll, sting. I squeeze my eyes shut, see flashes, chop blind.

At 2 a.m. in Budapest, we see a Slovenian dressed like an alien. He has on antennae with a chin strap. He tells us his father had a pen pal for thirty years and when they met, they got married. He asks Gwen to be his pen pal. He wants baby aliens with her eyes.

A black-haired boy with a sunken, haunted face in my art class always leaves the eyes in his drawings blank. It's more than a blank stare, it's deeper than bone.

I keep breaking light bulbs. We drag each other's cigarettes. Gwen's afraid to light the gas stove. It's not me. She's the one on fire.

I dream I am a prostitute and drive a car with a license plate that says BITCH.

I pass two old ladies counting syringes under the bridge. They are at number 29.

There are days everything she touches breaks. The arbor crashes onto a cat. The clothes line snaps. When Gwen tries to fix it, the hammer head flies off and re-breaks her toe. Glass shatters, doors slam, she becomes wind.

8,000 cups of American coffee and 8,000 American cigarettes are not enough to make us be in America.

I've been studying my map of the USA. Places I want to go in Texas: Melvin, Edward's Plateau, Maleshoe, Rising Star, Cactus, Sunray, Winters, Bronte, Texas, Earth.

It is warm for October. We are walking along the Arno saying we never drink beer in the afternoon, and why not? When we look to the right, we see two ice-cold German beers sitting on the river wall. We pick them up and laugh. We are beginning to understand how to get what we want.

We are in a taxi near our apartment when we see a woman with a huge red wig hit the trash collector over the head. We get out of the taxi and the red wig woman gets in. Tomatoes fall out of our grocery bag and squash on the ground. I collect moments when other people are falling apart like gold.

I dream about him again. We are stealing vegetables from a market in Mexico. I awake with my alarm clock up my sleeve. By the Mediterranean I find soles of shoes and cats and dead fish and bones, knotted driftwood and rubber strips of tire. I think if he stood in front of the ocean with holes instead of eyes, he would look no different.

His eyes are a smear of seaweed in the sun through all of the coasts of Europe with their own ebb and tide, their own rise and set and pull. I understand that I am diminished like the horizon between sky and ocean at night, when all is one expanse of black.

We walk into the liquor store. It is a full moon in December. She picks up the biggest bottle of Jack Daniel's from the shelf and pulls out her parent's credit card to be used in case of emergencies. "This, Mom and Dad, is for fucking me up."

I am trying to remember all of the things my mother used to tell me. One day I am lying in bed and I get such a strong image of my mother that I begin to cry. I call her from a pay phone and she says, "I've been praying all day for you to call me."

My dad writes that he is growing old. So am I. I don't think it suits us. In class, I try to write poetry dedicated to making him feel 20.

My literature professor says I can't do my final paper comparing the rings of Dante's *Inferno* to the rooms of our apartment. It's a shame. My room falls under "traitor to friends and family."

OLD BONES

My marriage begins in the house where my parent's marriage ends. Ghosts in the walls, echoes in the floorboards, fingerprints in the paint. I see glimmers, projections of myself at two, at four, six, and eight running through the house naked in my mother's cowgirl boots, digging red clay out of the backyard, sitting on the floor furnace like it's a campfire.

How do you move home again, and then stay? How do you repair the house that was part of your first breaking? How do you make new memories in old rooms?

Put in new windows, scrape the wallpaper, paint the walls. Knock out rooms and ceilings. Let the structure of the house be rebuilt as the doctors and the babies rebuild your body.

Your husband lays down a brand new floor, board by board. He guts the kitchen, replaces countertops and appliances, updates the plumbing and electrical, plants grass, rose bushes, trees. He lays his hands on everything, imprinting his scent, leaving his mark. But will it ever really be his home, too?

Cut out the parts that are dead, drag out as much of the old furniture and books and clothes and toys from the attic as you can. Try to start new using the same old bones.

It is both a blessing and a curse to make something new out of something so old.

CHAPTER 3

Writing the Body

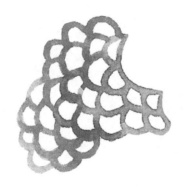

WRITING THE BODY

I believe writing comes as much from our bodies, our hearts, our guts, our throats, our chests, as from the thoughts formulated in our minds.

When I am tired or sick or in pain I can't write through to another level of story before I acknowledge the immediate sensations in my physical self. When my body has something it needs to say I'm not going to get very far doing anything else until I am willing to listen. And I can trust, when I'm writing or reading, that the sensations in my body tell me something I need to know. The quickened pulse, the sting of tears, the flush of heat, the goosebumps that cover me from head to toe, they all have something important to share.

The stories of our bodies can create the narratives of our lives. My beautiful, empathic student with Type 1 Diabetes who has been aware of her own mortality since she was a child and is now studying and practicing narrative medicine. The soft-spoken teacher with the failing pancreas who is putting herself first in her own life by writing the story of all she has survived. The wise and brave badass warrior woman whose cancer comes and goes and comes back again who lives completely in the moment.

Students with PTSD who have survived child abuse or domestic violence. Those of us overcoming and struggling with body shame and dysmorphia and self-loathing trying to understand who we really are. The survivors of sexual assault and abuse who are reclaiming their bodies, their voices, their stories, and their lives. Those whose bodies have birthed and lost babies, those who have grieved not being able to have babies at all. The process of aging. The transformation from maiden to crone, from young man to old, how we process life and death as it manifests through our physical forms.

My body has lost battles and won wars. I am earning its trust and it is earning mine. We are writing our way through, together.

MOUNTAIN BABY

"Hey little lady, I want to bite your titty," says Elmer, passing me a flask. He is one of two cowboys sent to carry me up the mountain to the dude ranch in Colorado's Flat Tops Wilderness Area where I've accepted the position of cabin girl. I've just graduated college and want to get as far away from the world of academia as possible.

"We don't talk to girls that way," says the other wrangler, Big Will, turning up Janis Joplin on the radio as we bounce and bang up the achingly gorgeous mountainside, turning onto Coffee Pot Road and beginning the long drive into the Flat Tops Wilderness Area. "Freedom's just another word for nothing left to lose," wails Janis and I try to settle in between these two new wild men.

Long after the sun has set, we pull up between the lodge and a spattering of cabins. "This way, Valley Girl," says Big Will, a mountain of a man who carries my army duffle bag into the black night like it's a bundle of feathers as coyotes howl in the distance.

The girls' cabin has a wood stove, a sink with ice cold water, a toilet, an oil lamp and two single beds piled high with old woolen blankets. The other cabin "girl" is a Lakota Sioux Indian woman named Kathy who gives me a medicine wheel that I hang in my window for protection, wondering how much I'll need it.

In the lodge before the sun is up, Kathy lights a fire in the woodstove and shows me how to make cowboy coffee, pouring water over the grounds in a silver kettle on top of the woodstove and when it boils, pouring a cup of cold water on top. I add enough sugar to make it sweet and learn to chew or spit the grounds that won't settle.

Kathy and I set the tables, clean the oil lamps, scrub and sweep the floors, steep the sun tea out on the porch, and launder all the towels and sheets on the mountain in a wringer-washer washing machine out by the generator that produces electricity for the lodge just a few hours a day. The wringer-washer remains more mysterious to me than the works of Nietzsche.

I struggle to master its machinations and fail—rusty hoses shoot from their moorings like snakes from Medusa's head, pounding me in the face with streams of dirty bleach water.

On my break in a rocking chair on the back porch staring across the mountains, I start to flick a cigarette but Elmer grabs my hand. "This is God's country, Cowgirl," he says. "Don't fuck it up." For the rest of the season I keep the butts in my pocket.

Even though I've been riding once, I'm still scared of horses. But I want to live in the wild and play with the big boys so on the second day when Big Will asks if I'd like to go for a ride, I say "Sure," like it's no big deal. Back in Denver I'd bought a shiny pair of hundred-dollar black leather boots that seem prissy and inadequate as I pull them on along with a second bra. I stuff my pockets with a lighter and cigarettes, knowing I am a fool to think Big Will will go slow enough to sustain fire. In the barn, he shows me how to spread out the blankets and then saddle Hooker, the same horse I rode last summer with Jenne. Big Will claims she's tame, but I know she's not and my heart pounds as I hoist myself up by the stirrups, throwing a leg over her broad back. Big Will waits patiently for me on Lightning, a horse reserved for the wranglers, as I try with every tensed muscle in my body to look natural.

"Don't let her know you're scared," he says with a laugh. "And another thing," he says, suddenly looking more like a boy than a man. "Hold on like hell. GIDDYAP!" he shouts then, digging his heels into the meaty flesh of Lightning's belly. Hooker doesn't wait for any sign of encouragement from me and the two horses bolt like race stock out of the corral and into the meadow, filthy with purple and red and orange wildflowers. In seconds we are across a field that takes twenty minutes to walk, shooting across a creek coursing with turgid black water, and then up and down the embankment and through the far pasture.

Big Will is a blur in front of me, bobbing up and down on his horse like he does this every day of his life. Ears flat and head down, Hooker shoots past Lightning and I crouch low, closing my eyes and keeping myself looser than I've ever been, so closely attached to another living thing.

When Hooker pulls us through a thicket of brambles, tiny thorns tear at the flimsy fabric covering my arms, branding me with a hundred little scratches and I finally forget how afraid I am and the danger and instructions and rules of riding shake free. Big Will hoots and whistles in front of and behind and beside me and I think holy hell, I am fucking flying.

My inner thighs are sore for days. The power, the thrill, the loss of control, the adrenaline, the mount and the dismount of the horse remains in my flesh and muscle and skin, forcing me to consider for the first time since leaving home that I inhabit the body of a woman.

Kathy says when I'm asleep I make shadow puppets with my fingers against the wall of the log cabin in the light of the oil lamp. She tells me I'm special and I look at the medicine wheel she gave me. The intricate, slender knots remind me of the spider webs in the rafters she won't knock out with the broom until she is forced to by the owner. "Such bad luck," she shakes her head sadly.

I love Kathy and she loves me until she comes into our cabin one afternoon and finds Big Will next to me in the narrow twin bed beneath my hoard of woolen blankets. Even though I beg and plead with her, she is cold and angry. I buy her silver hoop earrings in Denver to try to make up for sleeping with a man but when Big Will becomes my boyfriend, Kathy turns her head away when I look at her and Janelle becomes my only friend.

Janelle smacks her gum and carries at least four different shades of lip gloss in her pocket, even when we are on our knees scrubbing the floor in the bathroom. Our knuckles scald with hot water and bleach but she keeps the rings on her fingers anyway. She is a tiny thing in constant motion. Her thin golden hair is shimmery and bewitching as she swishes it around her shoulders, her voice brassy and bossy and loud. Janelle moves into the bunkhouse with Elmer after knowing him exactly one day.

On our short breaks between scrubbing piles of dishes and hauling dirty sheets from the cabins Janelle and I listen to Patsy Cline and Nanci Griffith and chain-smoke cigarettes.

She blows smoke through her shiny pursed lips into the open, waiting mouth of her dog Missy who laps up the smoke greedily with her soft pink tongue. Janelle gives everyone hell, refuses to follow direct orders and shows up to the kitchen in the morning when she feels like it. I love and hate her for it. We're all trying to survive out here in the wilderness, any way we can.

We are nestled in a valley blanketed with wildflowers and aspens and oaks next to the White Water River and all the wranglers are grizzled and handsome and foul-mouthed but from the start Big Will offers to help me with my chores. He doesn't blink when I streak his dark blue Wranglers with white strips of bleach. When he bounds down the mountain on his horse after a long pack ride with the other wranglers he brings bouquets of wildflowers for me.

At night we sing songs and drink beers around the campfire or play poker in the bunkhouse. I have no poker face but I learn to hold my cards closer to my chest and bet it all when I have a sure thing.

One night during five-card draw, the cook, a skinny ex-junkie, bursts through the bunkhouse door distraught. His chow mix, Calamity Jane, has been quilled by a porcupine. Slender daggers spring out of her huge brown fur coat, the tender flesh of her nose and her jowls. Big Will finds a pair of pliers and wrenches the quills out one by one while the other wranglers hold her down. I admire what he is able to do with his massive hands.

When I am sick with fever he brings me rosehip and chamomile tea as I toss and turn and sweat in my bed and as soon as I am better I let him join me under the covers and stay there for good.

Mid-season it's decided that the wranglers and kitchen staff will switch places for a day, that we will do their work and they will do ours so everyone will quit bitching and see how the other half lives.

My palms tingle and sweat as I make my way across the far pasture to jingle the horses, bring them into the corral for breakfast, a job rotated between wranglers, and now suddenly, all mine. But my first and favorite horse, Hooker, has moon blindness and has been quarantined with a blindfold over her eyes behind the stable.

Instead I have to ride Ace, a horse I barely know at all. Everything is new and bright and terrifying as I mount his back and set off on my own.

My mind freezes as I try to remember the knot to secure Ace to the tree that Big Will has shown me a hundred times. I imagine myself returning to the lodge defeated, forced to admit failure, that I can't do what the men can. I think of the Pussy Posse, a band of big-haired, brassy-mouthed women that came to the lodge last week to ride hard and screw wranglers and how I felt like I didn't belong with them either. At last my hands remember the knot and I experience the exhilaration of doing something with my entire body, riding hard and getting my boots dirty, all before breakfast.

Over eggs and bacon and grits and biscuits the wranglers are gloating too, but only because they haven't stripped the beds of the dirty sheets before covering them over with the new.

I am wearing yellow rubber gloves and dirty blue jeans and my hair is in a messy bun no less wild than the snakes on Medusa's head as I wrestle the hoses of the wringer washer when Big Will gets down on one knee amidst the suds on the wooden deck and asks me to marry him. "And," he says, "if you don't say yes today, I'll ask you again tomorrow."

"Okay then, no," I say intrigued by the promise and the threat. We have been moving from cabin to cabin, whichever is unoccupied, or the barn or the public showers or the bunkhouse to have sex while the other wranglers are out on a ride. I love the denim and leather dress he bought me in Denver, the birdhouse he painted with a sunflower, and the field he named after me on his farthest ride but I don't know if I want to be his wife. He calls me baby but when he writes my name he spells it wrong. I am 22. I don't know if I want to marry anyone.

The next day as I scour the mountain of dishes he circles my waist with his arms and asks me again. "Okay," I say. "But let's not tell anyone." He gives me the ring from his first marriage wrapped with tape so it will fit around my finger.

That night in Cabin Two, our clothes catch fire next to the burning woodstove and the cabin fills with black smoke. Big Will throws the ball of fire out the door and it sizzles in the frost, my new dress and one of two bras I have on the mountain burned to ash. I wrap myself in a blanket and run across the field back to the girls' cabin to try to find something else to keep me covered. Instead of selling the boxes of wine we are meant to serve the customers, the mother of the boss and I drink them all ourselves. Big Will is gone on longer pack rides that keep him away for days and I feel he has taken all the joy I brought up the mountain out there with him. While I used to take hikes or sketch the wranglers chopping wood or write or listen to music on my breaks, now all I want to do is curl up and sleep. Or drink. Tammy and I get high on our breaks with the skinny ex-junkie cook in his trailer in the woods.

One morning after I've finished making the beds Elmer finds me and says, "I'm sorry Cowgirl, Hooker didn't make it, they've taken her out to the far pasture." My eyes sting with tears and that afternoon I stash a beer in my apron pocket and set out across the fields to find her. A storm rolls in across the endless sky and I feel like I am the only person left alive in all of Colorado as I make my way across the valley.

I do find Hooker, but the vultures and flies have found her first. She is already a rotting carcass all alone in the tall grass, wildflowers grown up around her. I sit on a fallen log and open a beer, flies buzzing around her body.

IS THAT ME?

I have rarely been able to get even the slightest handle on what I look like. When my husband and I are out, be it at the mall or the museum, I set my sights on someone in the distance and whisper, "Is that me?"

"Yes" or "no," he whispers back and I nod gratefully as if by process of elimination we will eventually narrow down the entire world woman by woman, until at last I find myself looking back. Sometimes he'll give me a preemptive "NO!" before I even ask. "That's NOT you," he'll say. But how can I know for sure?

Mirrors and photographs lie. And my brain not only lies, it gives me contradictory lies. In fact I'm pretty sure my brain wants to keep me so preoccupied with wondering what I look like that I'll never get anything else done at all. Because, other than the horror of being hideous fundamentally programmed into every woman I know regardless of how she actually looks, what does it matter? A friend of mine tells me she's tired of being judged by the men who look at her. Frankly, I'm just tired of judging myself.

During my massage this week I thought how deeply intimate it was to lie naked on a table and let someone touch me while my eyes were closed and hers were not. What did she see, stretched out before her? It could have been anything from the Venus of Willendorf to Tinkerbell to The Thing. Who knows? Not me. I forced myself to relax into her loving, healing touch because I needed to release the acute pain in my right hip more than I needed to come off as a supermodel cheerleader slathered in almond oil. "Your body knows exactly what it needs," she told me when it was over. And it was miraculously true. My hip had released the pain. My body, yes. But my mind?

A friend told me she hates having her photo taken when she's traveling because it jolts her out of the experience unfolding within. I took a yoga class with her once where she instructed us to keep our eyes closed and move in faith into the darkness. It was beautiful and moving and part of me wished I could go on living in the dark forever. But I can't. It turns out that for at least half of the day, of my life, I must live in the light.

Yesterday I spent 30 minutes looking at old and new pictures of myself trying to make sense of the gap. The gap between how I looked then and how I look now. The gap between how I thought I looked then and how I know I looked then, now, looking back. A fifty-pound gap. A six-size gap. The current pictures tell a truth I haven't fully accepted. Writing helps me get closer to that truth. Writing helps me more fully accept and understand the me that I was and have become.

THE WAY I FEEL ABOUT MY WRITING IS THE WAY I FEEL ABOUT MYSELF

This summer I made an earth-shattering and also completely obvious discovery. After a decade of teaching creative writing to adults and kids, it has finally become clear to me that how we feel about our writing is how we feel about ourselves. Rarely do we love ourselves but hate our writing. Rarely do we hate our writing but love ourselves. When we say our writing is trite, boring, self-indulgent, or dumb, it's generally not the words on the page we are actually referring to.

As I work on letting my writing be, I'm working on letting myself and my life and my body be. As I work on letting myself be, I'm working on letting my writing be. When I surrender to the process of my writing, I surrender to the process of my life.

Last month my co-editor Sarah and I were going on television to promote our new book, *Nine Lives: A Life in 10 Minutes Anthology.* I was afraid to wear my sleeveless dress without a sweater into the interview, afraid that my dreaded armpit under-hang would steal the show. "If you put a sweater on over that sleeveless dress," Sarah told me point-blank in the parking lot, "you are letting the patriarchy win."

And I can't do that. Not for my sisters or mothers or students or friends. Not for my son growing up in this crazy world.

Not for myself.

And so, as a continued commitment to loving myself and fighting the patriarchy, this summer I am not wearing a potato sack with a skirt into the pool. I am not wearing a parka and cargo pants to hang out with friends when it's one million degrees. I am wearing fitted bathing suits, spaghetti strap tank tops and, when I feel like it, booty shorts.

And though I haven't quite yet achieved perfect self-love or finished smashing the patriarchy, I am doing my best to let my writing hang out and shake it all around. Allowing myself to be and allowing my writing to be go hand in hand.

CHAPTER 4

Writing Addiction

WRITING ADDICTION

When I was little I held AA meetings with my stuffed animals. "Just for today, I'm going to be good," said Papa Smurf. Charlie McCarthy, the marionette, was always trying to quit smoking. Snoopy was taking it "one day at a time." At eight I called my best friend and told her I was going to be her sponsor. My mother's business revolved around making buttons with inspirational slogans for people in recovery and I'd grown up with coloring books and crayons in the back of smoky AA meetings. We traveled to AA, NA and ACOA conventions in the United States, Mexico, and Canada in her Dodge minivan, often camping out along the way.

At 13, I swore I'd never become an alcoholic or an addict myself. I wrote an article for a local teen mag about breaking the cycle of addiction. That year I won the Creativity Award for my high school, the one trophy I've ever received in my life. I didn't want alcohol or drugs to interfere with my creativity. At 14, when I had my first sip of Boone's Farm Strawberry Hill, I fell deeply, strongly, madly in love.

As it turns out, I have an addictive personality and can get sucked in and under by just about anything. Credit cards, glazed doughnuts, drugs, alcohol, cigarettes, bad boys, and codependent relationships have all brought me to my knees. Learning how to turn my impulses for destruction towards creation has been the journey of this lifetime.

Writing my addictions hasn't fixed them or cured them, but it has helped me get through them. Writing helps me process, understand, excavate, and resurface. I have dozens of journals dedicated to the underworld of disease and darkness in a hundred different manifestations. But those journals are full of recovery too, the healing, the light, the a-has, the discoveries. Writing has been a lifeline that has helped me crawl my way up out of hell and pulled me back onto the land with the living.

Addiction manifests in many different ways. We might be addicted to substances or to people or to ways of thinking. We might be addicted to thoughts or behaviors or distractions. What addictions do you need to write your way through?

WRITING SOBER

For a long time, I didn't think it would be possible, and certainly not desirable, to write sober. At the very least, all of the great writers drank. Some did drugs or killed themselves too. Drinking was a minimum requirement for greatness. True writing came from a glorious darkness. Without a remarkable level of excess and debauchery there really couldn't be that much to say.

I stayed up late into the night drinking and writing, writing and drinking, and eventually writing and drinking and crying until soon it was just drinking and crying while the writing pretty much vanished altogether. Four in the morning was the most important time of day for me — reaching it was the pinnacle of writerly loneliness. I wrote many profound thoughts during the 4 A.M. witching hour, stories and secrets, all of which were illegible gibberish in the clear light of day.

When I got sober at 23, I was convinced I was giving up my dream of being a writer along with the Schlitz Malt Liquor and Mad Dog 20/20. Without the fuel of mood-altering substances I didn't know what I had to write. My brain was a blank piece of paper and alcohol was the match. I mourned the loss of everything I had known or hoped when I stopped actively destroying my life. I didn't know it, but it was in the depth of that grief that my true writing began.

The first year of my sobriety I had to give up everything cultural. I couldn't go to a play, plays made me want to drink. I couldn't listen to music. Music really made me want to drink. I couldn't read poetry or try to write anything with form or narrative or structure. The only thing I could write was feeling. Feeling, feeling, feeling. Writing carried and contained my feelings for months when nothing else could come out of me besides rage and fear, sorrow and grief. Writing was more of a bandage and a stretcher than a path to glory or publication. I leaned on it heavily, with my life.

I did feel a major gulf between my own life and the life of a writer for several years more. Basic survival was more important than researching literary magazines. Work, money, food, shelter, recovery, driving, living, and crying took precedence.

When writing returned, our relationship was different. There is now, in some ways, less romance, mystery, and intrigue. Writing sober is more raw, real, vital, and immediate than writing drunk. Writing and drinking is like going to a masquerade ball in a candle-lit banquet hall and waking up the next morning hungover in bed with a hideous creep you'd thought the night before was Prince Charming. Writing sober, what you see and what you feel is what you get.

WRITING FOOD

We drink from our mother's breast, or from a bottle. We were fed when we were hungry or we were allowed to stay hungry too long. We discovered the world of food as we grew, introduced to new flavors, new cultures, new temperatures, new textures, new ways of experiencing the world.

We were nourished, we learn how to nourish ourselves, we learn how to nourish others. Our bodies are made up of the bits and pieces we put inside of them. Food is connected to our most intimate caretakers — or the absence of them. To our grandparents, our friends, our children, our cultures, our religions.

Because it activates all of the senses at once, writing about food is a direct way to enter into certain times or characters of our lives. I can touch, feel, smell, and taste Great Aunt Eva's rhubarb pie that she served when we visited her in New Jersey and how she'd say, "You'd be such a pretty girl if you could do something with that hair." The Italian family I lived with for a month when I was 20 served me fresh apricot jam on hard Tuscan toast with a cup of espresso and cream for breakfast every morning. As a new, exhausted, and broke mother, there were a lot of nights we ate angel hair noodles with olive oil and sprinkled on Parmesan cheese.

We might be emotional eaters or use food as medicine for healing. We may be deprived or overindulgent. Food can represent comfort, safety or danger. Think of the pomegranate Persephone ate seed by seed in Hades.

Whether we hunt for food, buy it at a farmers market, or at 7-Eleven, the food we eat has a story to tell. Our lives can be remembered in meals, in kitchens, in gardens, or in grocery stores. Adding food into the pieces we are writing about our childhood or marriage or travels abroad adds texture and flavor to our writing. Think strawberries drizzled in hot dark chocolate. Think a can of Spam. The stories they tell are very different.

What did you have for dinner last night? Who ate it with you? What food do you dream about or crave right now? How do certain foods make you feel? The way to the heart may be through the stomach and I believe it can be the way into the heart of writing too.

HUNGER

My parents are hungry all the time, but for different things. My mom wants to make art and talk about books and eat steamed kale and rice cakes and gray bricks of tofu and foot-long sticks of celery. My dad wants to enjoy life, to go exploring and live it up. He loves cheeseburgers and pizza, fried chicken and microwaveable TV dinners that we eat in front of *Buck Rogers* and *The A-Team* and *The Wild Wild West* on his tube TV. He lets me choose between Dunkin' Donuts or Baskin Robbins on Wednesday nights when we go people-watching at the mall. In the morning, he brings me hot mugs of children's coffee: milk, honey, and a tablespoon of strong drip coffee. It tastes like mother's milk, like life.

My mom's mom died of diabetes when I was two and my mom was 31. Grandma Margaret had her toes cut off and then her legs and when she died she was in a wheelchair and I don't remember any of it. My mom swears she won't let the same thing happen to her or to me.

I travel back and forth between my parents, always hungry for the thing I don't currently have at the time. My mom or my dad, dessert or a dinner cooked at home. They both love me so much but I'd like to be everything to both of them at the same time: husband, wife, daughter, mother, child, queen.

My mother looks in the mirror and calls herself fat. She looks at me and says I'm beautiful. I suck in my stomach and wish I could cut the rolls off my thighs. I wait for my dad to come pick me up and take me to Wendy's, Arby's, the mall, so I can feel loved and special and treated and full. He tells me I'm smart and thoughtful and creative and funny. He tells me my hands are so steady I could be a surgeon one day. He tells me I'm clever and my mom tells me I can be anything I want to be when I grow up.

When I grow up I want to have a pretty face and perfect rail-thin thighs.

WRITING MONEY

We're not supposed to talk about money in polite company which makes it all the more important that we write about it. Each of us has a lifelong relationship with money, whether we grew up rich or poor, whether we are currently loaded or broke. We may support ourselves or we may be supported by someone else. We may feel strong and independent or indebted, kept, and bound. We may feel guilty for having too much money or ashamed that we don't have enough. The amount of money in our bank accounts and how we spend it has a story to tell. Writing about money is a way to write about who we've been and who we have become.

When I was growing up, sometimes the electricity would get turned off at my mom's house while my dad and I hunted for our furniture in the alleys downtown. I scrounged lunch money out of couch cushions even though my mom and I lived in the West End, one of the most affluent neighborhoods in Richmond. We were on welfare and food stamps, I had a reduced lunch ticket, and I shopped at thrift stores and yard sales, but we also traveled all over the country in my mom's used Dodge minivan. We went to museums and art openings and the theatre. My mom has had her own business making inspirational buttons for over 30 years and has won the Survivor of the Year award from the Richmond Chamber of Commerce. She also had a button on her dresser that read "Fuck the Real World, I'm an Artist." From my mother I learned that the pursuit of art and culture was far superior to the pursuit of money or security.

With the help of scholarships, grants, and a government loan I'm still paying off, I went to the second most expensive college in the country in 1997. I worked for minimum wage at the local movie theatre while the French millionaire I was in love with occasionally borrowed money from me when his ran out. He told me I had an emotional relationship with money when I asked him to pay me back. And I did. I'd gone from feeling scrappy and resourceful in Virginia to dirty, poor, and never good enough in New York. I couldn't achieve the heady sophistication of my wealthy, slender, blond, intellectual friends who flew around the world for fun.

The first time I got paid to write I was 29 and pregnant with my son. I took a photo of the check and laminated the article at Kinko's. Fifty dollars wasn't enough to pay a utility bill but it was better than winning the lottery to me. After getting laid off from the job I had at a local alternative weekly during the recession of 2008, I turned down the offer of a full-time job with benefits writing ad copy. I was afraid it would kill my soul. I kept this a secret from my husband for months. I cried at Target because I couldn't afford sunscreen for my son.

A warrant to appear in court was taped to my front door after getting sued by not one but two credit card companies. Making a phone call to ask for help and then accepting the help that was offered took all the strength I had. And that was the bottom from which I've slowly rebuilt. I now open every bill, answer every call, repay my debts one by one. Taking creative risks, putting my work out into the world, believing in my own intrinsic value and worth, is the story money now tells about me.

How does money wind its way through your life? What stories does it have to tell?

BRONXVILLE THEATRE

I carry body bags of bright yellow popcorn back to my dorm room after my night shift at the Bronxville Movie Theatre where I work the candy counter. Me and the girls in my hall eat it by the fistful as if we have no mothers, as if there's no God, as if there can be no evidence left in the morning.

I pump fake butter into popcorn and hand over Milk Duds and Twizzlers to New York's finest. George, my boss, sends all of his money back home to India. The ticket seller, Edna from Yonkers, is a short round loud-mouthed redneck who is madly in love with George. I pour vodka into courtesy cups of Sprite and read Dostoevsky while leaning against the hot popcorn case or talk to the cabbies between shows. I almost make enough to cover my phone bill and the Marlboro Reds I chain-smoke on my breaks.

I bring my friends to movies for free on my nights off but when the boy I love comes in with a girl and George waves them in past the ticket counter, I stand humiliated in my uniform, hot tears spilling onto the candy counter. Edna comes over and rubs my back through my polyester uniform with her small fat starfish hands. Her heart is broken all of the time, too.

WRITING SEX

I have never had much luck writing about sex without falling to cliché or awkward, clumsy words and phrases that feel more like junior high kids clunking around in the dark than lovers in a passionate tryst.

I have found, however, that you can write about sex without describing the actual act. Sex has as many definitions as love, as many ways to write about it as there are people doing it.

We can write about sex as love, or sex as a weapon. We can write about sex as assault or abuse or punishment. As romance or experiment. As exploration or discovery. We can write about sex as the forbidden and taboo or the mundane and ordinary.

We can write about sex as the genesis of new life or the beginning of an affair. We can write about sex that stays within or crosses or defies gender. We can write about sex as stereotype or self-definition, within marriage or after divorce. Sex as sin or salvation.

There are so many ways to write about sex. To further character, to further plot, as political analysis. Sex as a practical act, a spiritual union, a non-verbal contract. Body to body communication.

I was conceived in a tent in the Shenandoah Valley on my mother's birthday. My son was conceived the day after Valentine's Day because after exhausting ourselves at the climbing gym on February 14th, my husband and I both passed out on the bathroom floor. Sex is the beginning of life but it doesn't end there.

What part does sex play in your story? How has sex shaped your character or changed the plot of your personal narrative?

SUN GOD

On the first day of school at the reception on the fancy, manicured lawn I see the Sun God. Tall, blonde and tan with ocean-green eyes. "Oh you're just another Goldmund, aren't you?" I say. I'm on a major Hermann Hesse kick and certain my reference will float over his head.

"I think he was a bit more philandering than I," the Sun God says, and in that moment he is mine and I am his but I'm the only one of the two of us who knows it. The only one bound by the gut with a longing for him.

He tells me, eventually, after we've been friends for a while — staying up all night, wandering the streets, drinking whiskey until we pass out drunk — that he is going to buy a notebook to write down everything I do, everything I say, everything I wear. He can't believe I'm Jewish, that I dress in clothes from the thrift store, that I'm on scholarship, that compared to his, my parents are poor. He comes from a château in the south of France. His room was a chapel on the land and he looks like a prince wrapped in silk, shocked to discover the customs of the natives in this new land.

He says my hands are clammy like rosebuds, that he'd think my mouth was sexy if he didn't know it was mine. I dream about him every single night, call him Little Bit, memorize his accent, the color of his throat, his perfect hands. When we finally sleep together it's like we are breaking up, breaking apart. He rips down my tights and pulls up my dress, refusing to kiss me on the mouth or anywhere at all. Afterwards, when he passes me on campus, he pretends he doesn't know me, that I could be anyone at all.

EVERYTHING I COULD

The first time I held a gun was in the car of a married man I'd met at wedding. I was 19, home from college, heartbroken, and desperate to feel wanted by anyone at all. Thirty-five, rail-thin with black hair and eyes, he slipped me Dixie cups of white wine right under my father's nose. He looked like Skeletor, or a used car salesman. Later that week he looked me up in the phone book.

What do I have to lose? was my attitude as we drank margaritas at a Mexican restaurant. He pulled his wedding ring out of his pocket and placed it between us on the table. I laughed it off; I laughed at all of it, an enormous joke separating me from the depths of my unwantedness. The French boy I'd loved so desperately in college had taken my hair out of its barrette and called me his greatest enemy. As I'd leaned over him he'd turned his head and refused to say another word.

In the car, the man reached under the front seat and pulled out a pistol, placing the solid, cold weight of it in my hand. I held it like it was a dying animal, like it was my responsibility to keep it somehow alive. The man parked, took his gun, put it away, and led me through the courtyard of a church. I sat next to him on a bench surrounded by roses and moonlight and then he put himself in my hand, hard and hot, and I did what I could to end the scene unfolding in front of me, a scene I wanted to write about more than I wanted to live. The boy had said he'd think my lips were beautiful if he didn't know they were mine. How could I bridge the chasm of self between the girl I was and the girl someone else could love?

Right now I'm both that 19-year-old girl and this 42-year-old woman, walking hand in hand, talking it through, flushing it out. The girl tells me she didn't always do the healthiest, safest, smartest things to survive, and I tell her it's OK, she did everything she could.

CHAPTER 5

Writing Grief

WRITING GRIEF

Writing grief is one way to help survive the experiencing of it. It's a way of staying grounded when oceans of feeling threaten to wash us away. It's a way to transform the unbearable and ineffable into something solid, something tangible, something we can begin to wrap our minds around.

Writing has helped me wade through messy, explosive grief. Sometimes I can only write out raw pain, but sometimes that pain takes shape, forming a raft I can rest on. My friend Tim recently wrote a poem about grief as a wave that captured the feeling for me in a complete and perfect way.

When I was going through my series of miscarriages, the most gutting, blinding grief I've experienced in my life so far, I was exhausted, angry, numb, weepy, and erratic. The ability to capture even tiny moments of that pain lightened some of the heavy darkness in my heart. If I could somehow explain how bad it was, I felt a little better. If I'd had the choice, I would have traded all of the writing in the world for any one of those lost babies. But since it wasn't a choice, the pieces I wrote about them were what I had to hang on to. Those lines of writing from that time are precious to me still.

Who or what have you lost that was important to you? How was your life different before and after? Describe the way grief feels in your body.

WAVE

Grief is a wave
that never breaks but
always runs right through you.

People whose hearts are in the right place
say it comes less and less often —
that it comes with less wasting horror

but you may as well know
they're deluding
themselves —

The waves will keep coming.
They'll always undo you.
If there's a trick to survival

it's getting used
to coming
Undone.

— Tim McCready

WRITING YOUR OWN DEATH

I have a student who is dying. She entered hospice this week and is now on oxygen four times a day. She doesn't know how much longer she has to live, but her breath is short and tight and she finds it difficult to walk up the stairs. Her children are 14 and 17. She longs to see her daughter graduate from high school, to witness her son's developing sense of humor. She is young, she is beautiful, looks young and healthy. She is in her forties, just a few years older than me.

She told me that when she started taking my class she was determined not to write about her cancer. She didn't want to be known as Cancer Girl. She didn't want the other writers to be horrified, or to hover over her, offering advice. But as her pen hit the page, despite her best intentions, the dam broke open. Rage and grief and longing and sorrow poured out of her pen. Her questions for God, her deep and wild love for her husband. Her wishes for her memorial service, her hopes for her children. The people who are able to meet her where she is, those who most achingly can not.

The stunning beauty and wild joy she finds in her every day. Nachos at a Mexican restaurant. A hot bath. Her adorable pug. Real Coke. Every minute with her family. The decision to let go of negative, unsupportive people and surround herself with love, care, and authenticity. She writes for herself, for her legacy, to capture her spirit and her love and give it as a most precious gift to those she leaves behind.

WRITING IS SOMETHING WE CAN DO WHEN THERE'S NOTHING ELSE THAT CAN BE DONE

When I get news that a beloved family member has a terminal illness, I wail like a wild animal. And then I call my oldest friend. "I don't think I'm made for this," I tell her. In October last year, my friend's own mother did the unthinkable and died. I watched mountains of grace and grief sweep through their family like I was watching a tsunami from just above, on a shaky ledge.

"Yes, you were made for this," my friend says. "You have always done things we never thought you could." She cites starting my own business and jogging and saving my marriage as examples. Her speech is impassioned and beautiful and makes me feel better, but underneath, I think we must both know she's lying. No one is made for this.

One fall, several years ago, two of my friends died tragic, sudden deaths two weeks apart. One on a motorcycle, the other in a fire. During the surreal, grief-stricken days after, it was all I could do to get up in the morning and make it through the day. I was a tangled, weeping mess of shock, loss, and powerlessness. There was only one thing I could do that saved me and helped them: writing. I was asked to write the obituary for one friend and a eulogy for the other. At the classes I taught during those difficult weeks, I wrote my heart out, and back in. The thread of writing helped stitch the broken, jagged days back together. I couldn't bring my friends back, take away the pain of their grieving loved ones, reverse time, or undo what had been done. But I could honor their spirits, transcribe their essence, and preserve their memories with words on the page.

I want to think I'll rise to every occasion, that God never gives us more than we can handle, that I'm made for all the moments I've been given. I want to think that I will be foraging for fire and food and friends and not wailing in a ditch or wringing my hands in the ruins of society.

Writing is something we can do when there's nothing else that can be done.

PROM QUEEN

Will Senior's cabin in Gateway, Arkansas, population 69, is so small that Big Will and I move into the tool shed. Our mattress is wedged between power saws and long-handled shovels and there is no plumbing or electricity. Home sweet home, I say, shoving my bag into a cobwebbed corner. At least we're not stuck in Richmond, I tell myself. At least I know that much.

Will Senior has a farm with an extensive vegetable garden with every manner of leafy green, groves of shiitakes, his own crop of marijuana and a barrel of walking sticks crowned with animal heads he has carved himself. We are in a dry county but he drives us to Ruby's Liquor Store across the line and we stock up on whiskey, beer, and Manischewitz wine, which he splashes with ginger ale to serve us his famous Blackberry Cadillac.

He has been a widower for one year. His third wife Linda choked to death on a chicken bone at the diner up the street and he blames himself for not saving her. I notice that the land and the cabin, grown over with weeds and dust, could use a woman's touch.

Our second week on the farm a foal is born and Big Will carries her across the pasture in his arms, her long legs akimbo. My baby, I think and we spend her first hours and days by her side trying to coax her to latch on to her mother.

When my mother calls I tell her how much I love my new life on the farm. "Oh Valley," she says, "how will you ever learn to live with just one man?"

When they tell me they are going to slaughter a goose for our supper, I decide to watch. I have never seen anything killed before, but I know that living on a farm requires certain sacrifices. Big Will grips the belly while his father steadies the neck. The goose does not go easily and Will Senior has to use his axe like a saw to get from one end of the neck to the other. I don't allow myself to blink until the last jagged blow when Will Senior slices through his own thumb. A stubby piece of flesh dangles from a thin flap of skin and I follow him into the kitchen where he sets the goose's feet on the counter.

I hold my breath, dumping cayenne pepper into his open vein as he instructs, watching his blood pump into the sink, mingling with the goose's before swirling down the drain. That night we eat goose breast for dinner, storing the legs in the freezer, wrapped in foil.

No one else on the farm is working so I get a job a few towns over at the Lodge on Whitney Mountain cleaning rooms and waiting tables. It's a five-star hotel and I have to wear a tuxedo but the washing machine at the farm is hooked up in the yard and there is no dryer so I hang my clothes on the porch to dry where they sway in the wind like a scarecrow. I come home from my shifts with my pockets stuffed with cash which we spend at Ruby's Liquor Store. The morning after I spend the whole night in the barn with the foal, Will Senior names her Morning Feather. "She's yours, Cowgirl" he says. "I want you to have her." She is by far the most beautiful and terrible gift I've ever received. Helpless over her beauty and her too-long legs, in my head I call her Prom Queen.

While Big Will sleeps in the afternoon, Will Senior and I saddle up the horse and the mule and take long rides through the countryside, galloping through the groves and orchards past old farm houses. I return with long scratches on my arms from the brambles which I wear proudly like war paint.

Big Will is like an extra appendage as his father and I perform the chores around the farm and care for the baby. When he tries to cut the grass with the riding lawn mower it sputters to a halt and dies for good. "You're like King Midas, son," says Will Senior. "Except everything you touch turns to shit." When Big Will reaches out for me on our mattress in the tool shed at night, I roll over and pretend to be asleep.

I draw the flowers along the fence line, write in my journal, and read. I go swimming with Melissa, the woman who paints gourds and has visions the next farm over and whose house, all unfinished beams and rafters, feels like the skeleton of a giant whale who's swallowed me whole. When we're in the quarry we don't see the copperhead snakes circling and winding around themselves until we pull ourselves, naked and dripping wet, onto the shore.

"Cowgirl," says Will Senior, "I need your help." He leads me into his bedroom and opens the closet, where all of his wife's clothes still hang as if she might come back and wear them again. "They've all got to go and I can't do it myself," he says. I am happy that he needs me so I gather garbage bags from the kitchen and begin to take stock of the pinks, blues, and yellows, the cottons, wools, and polyesters.

But instead of bagging them up, I try them on. Between the king-sized bed and the full-length mirror, I slip on blouses, Wranglers, and pink silk lingerie. I make a tidy stack on the bed of what fits, stuffing into the bag what doesn't. Last, on a shelf in the back of the closet, I find her wedding dress. It is pressed and perfect, preserved in its dry cleaner bag like a gift. I tug it on over my head and smile when the white lace hugs my curves in all the right places. I stare at myself in the mirror. The apparition of a bride stares back. I think about our two bodies, hers in the ground and mine emptier than it's ever been. This is what I would have looked like, I think, if I had married Big Will. I hope to God that I've made the right decision.

I keep Linda's lingerie and yellow raincoat but stuff the rest of her clothes into big black trash bags to take to Goodwill. When I tell Will Senior the job is done he gives me a pair of her ruby red earrings which hang from my ears like drops of blood.

After two months on the farm, Big Will tells us he has decided to visit his mother in California. He's already bought his Greyhound ticket and will be leaving in the morning. His dad and I take him to the station and when we drive back home he takes my hand in his.

"It's just us now, Cowgirl," he says and when we get back I go to check on the baby in the barn but her eyes are glassy like Christmas ornaments. I cry and sweat as we dig her grave and bury her underneath the elderberry tree. When she's in the ground I sleep in Will Senior's king-size bed, trying to forget the troubles of a girl beneath the weight of a man.

In the night I dream I've been buried alive. Dirt pours from my mouth, snakes writhe through the sockets of my eyes. When I wake up screaming Will Senior brings me a cup of tea and leads me out into the bright sun where I spend the morning in the cherry tree plucking shiny red globes until they fill my bucket. Then we boil a batch of cherries with sugar and orange peel. I ladle the mixture into jars labeled Bittersweet Summer Cherry Jam.

Big Will calls to talk to me and when I hang up the phone I sob into his father's shoulder. "He thinks I'm an angel that can do no wrong."

"That makes two of us, Cowgirl," Will Senior says and I know it won't be long before I leave him too.

WHAT TO KEEP AND WHAT TO GIVE AWAY

I decide to surprise my husband by painting our bedroom a deep burgundy. But I paint walls like I mow the lawn, in a haphazard pattern or with no pattern at all. I've chosen a red-purple the color of all those jugs of Carlo Rossi, wine I used to buy from the Getty Mart with my fake ID. Great patches of too-thick and then too-thin paint quilt the walls of a bedroom that while small already, now seems smaller, and darker too. These are the walls that kept me company, that I memorized while lying on our king-sized mattress on the floor during my two months of doctor-mandated bed rest.

Friends come, bring pot roasts, bundt cakes, watermelons, magazines, chocolate. They wash the dishes and vacuum my floors while Stan works and I stare at my own four sloppy horrible walls trying first to provide a safe, solid home for the baby I know is a girl, I know is me, that will save me from myself as I gag on prenatal vitamins and say prayers even to Jesus, even to the angels the psychic surgeon said I had. I am not sad, when, after we find out the baby will not be born alive, Stan re-paints the walls a bright, solid, streak-free white.

**

I'm 19 weeks along this time when the nurse is unable to find a heartbeat with her fetal monitor. "This happens sometimes," she says, but she is paging the doctor. The doctor can't find a heartbeat either.

They let me stay in the room as long as I need to try and gather myself. Office hours are over and they are packing up, ready to go. It is like my real life has stopped here, and the story of my life is about to begin. There are terrible decisions to be made. Do we hold a service or plant a tree? Do I allow them to take her remains or do I request to keep them, to see and to bury? In the end, they put me out and we save nothing.

It is impossible to go anywhere. I despise pregnant women. I avoid them like oozing lepers. I cross to the other side of the street, dart to the next aisle at the grocery. I give their fat bellies the evil eye, curse their able hips, turn my back on what looks to be easy, effortless bliss.

We fight over what to keep and what to give away. I want to put it all in the attic. I want to know it is there, safe, untouched, even if I never look at any of it again. But he wants to give it away, be rid of it, not have it hanging, literally, over our heads. One night at dinner, he offers a stroller to his co-worker whose wife is expecting their third child. "How dare you?" I seethe. I glare at them, push away from the table, refuse to return.

Friends sit on the edge of the bed, stop in unexpectedly, send cards, call throughout the day. It is not enough. It is all wrong. The words they say bend and fold and are packed away before I can open the door to watch them leave.

**

I am sitting at my desk when the bleeding begins again. I have a new job at a school for boys. The headmaster and his assistant are talking behind closed doors and I have been left in charge of the hallway. I should alert someone, shut down the computer, tidy my desk and return six or seven phone calls, but the sobs blooming in my chest send me home to bed, where I lie for the next two days.

My heart doesn't break, it simply slips between my legs. Stan brings me flowers and stays home from work for at least one day before returning to his routine. I discover that you can eat your weight in chocolate and still not feel better. The same holds true for salt and vinegar potato chips, Easy Mac Triple Cheese, and sugar cookies rolled in vanilla icing.

"I don't care, just do something, anything," I beg the young Korean hairdresser, who shrugs her shoulders and then aims the scissors at the back of my head. She snips soundlessly and I squeeze my eyes shut until she says "All done" and even then I barely dare to look. It is gone, all of it. My hair is cut close to the skull and I am happy. It is the desired effect. I don't recognize myself at all.

**

This time the doctor lets me leave out the back door without paying. I am weeping, hysterical, hiccuping. A black man is in the hall with his two small boys. He stops the elevator door with his shoulder and takes my hands in his massive fist. He bows his head in prayer. "Dear Jesus," he begins. And then "Jesus...something something...Jesus.

May the blood of Jesus wash over you," he mumbles in prayer. I have a vision of Jesus standing over me, his blood dripping down my head. I start to laugh. He can't tell. He thinks I'm still crying. He lets the elevator door go and I begin the descent. Thank you Jesus for making me laugh.

At an AA meeting a man weighing over 300 pounds tells me that my ancestors suffered so that I could have a better life. They were slaves in Egypt, settled in Israel, endured the Holocaust. "Your problems are small," he says. "Your worst fears haven't even happened." I want to slap him in the face. I want to scream, "Yes, they have."

The phone rings; I don't answer it. The phone rings; I don't answer it. The phone rings; I don't answer it. Take a message. She's not here. She's busy. She's preoccupied. She can't come to the phone. Do you want to leave a message?

"I haven't met any other writers in here," says Blessy, my IV nurse. I guess other writer's babies don't die, and if they do, they don't go to Henrico Doctor's Hospital to have them removed.

This is all part of God's plan I think. No, it isn't. Yes, it is.

**

I ask God why he didn't give me these babies. God says, My child, I did.

THE ART OF THE UGLY CRY

I am a crier. I cannot tell you the number of times I've cried my mascara off. Or laughed so hard I've started sobbing. Or cried during songs or movies or commercials or even the right tone of silence. In fact, a Finnish witch once said that in her country's magical hierarchy, I would be considered a Crier, one tasked with carrying the emotional weight of the village.

This struck me as apt although lately I've been crying a little less. I think it's the right combination of therapy, boundaries, and meds. I definitely still cry, just not for three days straight. I haven't sought out a parking lot just to cry in my car. For better or worse, crying has been a powerful tool in my healing journey.

My first year sober I cried every single day, sometimes the whole day long. I cried on walks, in coffee shops, pumping gas, buying Soy Dream at Kroger. The icebergs inside me were melting and the tears poured out of me like an avalanche.

Although I don't miss crying all the time, I see crying as a perfectly normal physical human reaction, like laughing or sweating. It keeps me emotionally current. If I build up a backlog of pain and tears I know I'm in trouble, but writing can help release it.

People often apologize for crying in class while they are writing or reading their pieces out loud. One beautiful new student wrote me an email after a workshop apologizing for crying while writing about the death of her child. "I was not raised to enter a room of strangers and make them feel uncomfortable. We save that misery for those closest to us in my family," she wrote. She told me she felt like a pony, wondering what she was doing in a house.

I wrote back to her from my seat on a charter bus to Arlington Cemetery for the burial service of another student's 19-year-old son who was killed in Afghanistan. I told her how this student cried frequently as she wrote about the life and death of her son and that those of us in class with her cried, too. How sometimes I teach whole classes through the tears that come up for me in my own writing.

I told her I was honored by her willingness to share her truth. "We're all horses wondering what the hell we're doing in the house," I said.

Surrender to your feelings. Allowing them to come through us onto the page is how we heal and how we write, at least if we want to write anything good.

CHAPTER 6
Writing to Heal

UNZIPPING

If you bring forth what is within you, what you bring forth will save you. If you do not bring forth what is within you, what you do not bring forth will destroy you.

— Jesus of Nazareth, Gospel of Thomas

I think of writing as a process of unzipping ourselves down the front, peeling back a layer of skin and letting our guts fall out onto the table. We expose what's hidden beneath the shiny, tough facade we present to the world. We reveal our insides, the beauty and the blood and the heart and guts of it.

Some of us feel unzipped writing about sexual abuse or betrayal. For some of us it's admitting a shortcoming or character flaw. For some students, writing about their messy house is as intimate as another person's exploration of their childhood abuse. One student wrote for weeks about her bathroom renovation before delving beneath the surface of her alcoholic family. Some students have written with gut-wrenching honesty about the scars on their bodies, their relationship with self-harm, and living with mental illness, while others reveal the uncertainty of starting a new job or a fight with a loved one. We don't have to use a scale of measurement to compare ourselves to anyone other than ourselves when we reveal what's boiling underneath.

Again and again, people in writing classes are shocked by the similarities, the overlaps, the threads that emerge from all of our own lives. Rarely does the composed-looking writer in the seat next to us look like the story of horror or redemption emerging from the page.

But when we are willing to unzip our skin, to be honest at the deepest level we can be, it's always a relief to see how much more similar, more human, more alive we are on the inside, despite how different and together we might look on the outside.

The stories I resonate with the most strongly don't require the removal of clothing so much as the removal of skin. When we reveal who we are beneath the surface, we find the stories we most need to write, and we write the stories we most need to heal.

NEVER GO TO HELL WITHOUT VIRGIL

When I was in Italy studying Dante's *Inferno,* I had a dream in which I was told: "Never go to Hell without Virgil." I have carried that wisdom with me ever since.

When we revisit monsters from our past, monsters that haunt us still, I think it's best we don't try to fight them alone. We need a guide or a muse to help us escape our monsters without being torn to shreds or sucked down under forever. My monster is handsome and vicious. Charming and smart. His tongue is a knife and his words cut through to the bone. My monster doesn't just tell me my writing is bad or boring or worthless, my monster tells me that I am bad and boring and worthless too.

I've met very few writers without monsters of their own. When I've had classes write and then share their monsters with the class, it's the stuff of nightmares and horror stories that fills the room. When we write out our monsters, our aim is not to kill them but to steal their power and use it for ourselves. When we look at our monsters directly and call them by name, they begin to lose their grip on us and we begin to be able to write straight through them, harnessing their power for ourselves.

But not being controlled by the terrible, negative voices in our heads might not be enough on its own. We might need to create positive, encouraging, and loving voices, too. One of my own students gave me the idea of creating a muse by introducing me to her own. Her muse was a beautiful red-headed witch that visited her in dreams. Sometimes I borrow her muse when I have trouble conjuring my own.

One wise friend told me that the voice in our head that shouts the loudest is not the voice we should be listening to. The quiet whisper of a voice has our best interest at heart. That voice can be our muse. My muse has taken the form of mentors, friends, teachers, readers, students, and the beautiful faces of those I trust enough to hold my work fiercely and gently in their hands and hearts. I think during a long-term writing process it's worthwhile to identify your monster and create your own muse.

The ancient Greeks had muses we can borrow from or we can create one of our own. Someone who wants you to tell your story and who will love you, approve of you, and affirm you while you do.

Everyone willing to lead me out of hell has been my muse. Therapists, sponsors, friends. Prayers and songs. The smile and nod and warmth of another writer able to hold my gaze after I've read. The brave woman who just spilled her guts onto the page assuring me it's safe for me to do the same. My muse is Me Too, Hell Yes, and Keep Going Girl, You've Got This.

THE FUEL OF FEELING

We do not have to arrive at writing practice in the perfect mood or even a good mood. We can come to the page with every and any feeling we have. We can show up angry, grieving, jealous, sad, confused, exhausted. We don't have to apologize for our feelings or explain them away. We can use them as fuel to drive our narrative forward, each feeling lending itself to a different kind of expression.

I believe that when we write tired we are often more vulnerable and have less energy to put up our usual filmy walls of resistance. Anger can add force to our words while sorrow might soften them. Each emotion brings a different aspect of our lives and ourselves to the page.

I have shown up to my notebook red hot with fury and doubled over in grief. I have entered the page confused, uncertain, unsure. Almost without fail, I emerge from my writing practice feeling differently than when I entered it. The physical, mental, emotional, and spiritual act of writing transmits and transforms emotion. The stories we write become carriers of those feelings, that, suffused into our words, can be felt by our reader.

We know when we read something fueled by emotion that was born in the heart or the body as opposed to a wholly clinical academic piece pried from the head. Our bodies respond when we read words written with the fuel of feeling. We don't have to turn away from the page because we aren't in the right mood. Every mood we have has something different to say, another piece to add to our story.

BAD VALLEY

After I had my baby, I tried to kill my dark side. Moms can't live in the shadow of the Underworld contemplating their inner demons and tossing back with Satan. Moms have to be awake, aware, alert, conscientious, and above all else, good. Besides, during those fertility years I didn't have much time to grapple with my dark side. There were too many prenatal vitamins and hormones and decisions about diapers. There was the terror of trying to keep something alive besides myself. There was the grief over my miscarriages and the heavy lifting of a marriage under the strain of the aftermath accompanying new life and sudden death.

When my son was born I reserved every ounce of writing energy I had for my freelance gigs. I nursed while I read and typed up my book reviews one-handed. I was in survival mode paid by the word. When my son was ready for preschool, to be in someone else's care an entire three hours a day, everything I'd tried to shove down came roaring back up.

I caught glimmers of her, tastes of her, I could smell her on the wind. But because I could no longer fully be her, I created her, my alter ego: Bad Valley. Bad Valley did all the things Good Valley could not, and she did them on the page. Bad Valley took night buses and went to bars. She could pick up and leave at the drop of a hat, wander, escape, smoke cigarettes in bed and eat nothing but candy all damn day.

I devoted blog post after blog post to Bad Valley, feeling the rush of exhilaration in living vicariously, creating something I could not fully have. But then Bad Valley became real, snaking her way out of my notebook and into my life and in giving myself to her I almost lost everything I had.

Integrating has been painful, beautiful, messy, and necessary. Bad Valley has a place now, on the page. I let her live and scream and travel and play when she needs to. She helps make me whole.

WRITE YOUR ALTER EGO

Write your alter ego. Resurrect an old discarded side of you. Invent the character you've always wished you could be. Rescue who you once were, and have lost, but miss still.

I invented Bad Valley as a release valve for the steam building up inside of me during the early compressed years of becoming a mother and wife. Where had I gone? Where was the wild girl I'd known so well? I wondered if she was gone forever but when I sat down to write, she poured out of my pen. Ours was a happy reunion.

Bad Valley took buses at night and rides from strangers. She was devil-may-care, throwing sense and caution to the wind. She had a wild heart for writing and reclaiming her essence helped restore a sacred lost part of me to me.

Creating our alter egos on the page is a satisfying way to give life to the voices in our heads, the remnants of lives we have lived, the shadows of the characters we could have been.

At my creative writing camps for kids we create our alter egos on the very first day and change them throughout the week, adding to their storyline, helping them evolve. Our alter egos are a gateway to fiction, to dreamscapes, to untapped realms of our imagination. Our alter egos can reveal shadow sides, hidden sides, stories within ourselves we have yet to live.

WILD THING

A few weeks ago, I visited my friend Edward in New York City. It had been far too many years since I'd seen him last and the aftershocks of old love made new have been reverberating through me like a tornado that arrived suddenly after all the other storms had passed. Old memories and new feelings have surged up and knocked me down like a toddler in a tidal wave. I don't know if it's bad or good or if there's anything to be done about it other than to stand up, to get the sand out of my hair and saltwater out of my mouth. The fish flapping in my bathing suit might be here to stay.

On the way to a writing retreat last weekend in the mountains of rural Virginia, I listened to his gorgeous, heart-wrenching mix tapes and CDs spanning 20 years and the music pried me open like an instrument plucked through from sound to soundlessness. A buried treasure unearthed, the shine and sparkle and gleam, blinding. Love blindness. Like an unexpected hug from a lion, a grizzly bear. Will it kill me to hug back? Will it kill me if I don't? Will I have to re-bury this love dug up fresh from its grave? Because even requited love can hurt. The first time you see the face of your child, you are suddenly aware of how much you have to lose. Can I allow myself to love someone with such wild abandon, with such little reservation knowing now all that I do?

Because our love existed in a suspended state of grace during the darkest years of my life, never spoiled by sex or the mundane hell of the day to day. Edward saw me when I was unseen, loved me when I was unloved, believed I could dance and hike and sing when I believed none of those things myself. He took me skinny dipping and camping and driving all over this country from one state to the next, over the rivers and through the hills, from the city to the wilderness and back again. He came down to Hell, stayed with me for a while and then pulled me out. How do you ever get over that? I'm pulling the heavy, velvet cloak of who we were tighter around my shoulders, wondering in which closet I can hang us now.

And that's the real work I'm doing here. Figuring out how to reassemble myself into a human woman, wife and mother without losing—or becoming—the girl I was.

I can't reinhabit that body or that life or that time, I have to have the patience to let who I am, who we are now, unfold. There is something eternal, bright, and beautiful about being a wild thing loved by a wild thing, even if we had to grow up and grow away and live in other places and get jobs and marry other people. I loved Edward's beautiful, kind, intelligent husband and he loved mine. We are who and where we are supposed to be, and my hope now is not to live or love in a suspended state of grace, but in a very present and timeless one.

While I can't relive the past I can write my way through it, write letters to it, write my way back from who I was to who I am, piecing all the parts of myself back together as I go.

HOW WE HELP

A couple of years ago, I taught a Life in 10 Minutes workshop at VCU, a hands-on experiential class aimed at helping teach stress-management skills to future physical therapists, nurses, and others entering the healthcare field. There were about 40 students, many ethnicities, mostly young but a few older, mostly women but a few men.

For the first 20 minutes I felt like an alien with three heads. My mouth was open but I didn't know what was coming out of it. I know I said I was in recovery from drugs and alcohol and perfectionism. I know I said writing had saved my life but I'd had to invent a different relationship with it, unlike any I'd had before. I know I asked them to be brave and vulnerable and to not judge their writing as it emerged on the page. Blank stares, empty faces, and a few polite smiles stared back. During the next ten minutes, I scribbled out the fear of tanking in my notebook as they wrote in theirs.

And then it was time to share. They were reluctant at first. A couple of brave souls read about how stressful it was to do well in school amidst the pressures and demands of everyday life. A long silence followed before I called on a young woman in the front row. "I can't believe I'm going to read this," she said. "I've never shared this with anyone," she said. "I want to help people but I don't know how," she said. And then she read her piece, shaking, crying, pausing between sentences to choke back sobs. The real time description of her rape was a punch in the gut, full of horror and pain, but beautifully, honestly, and powerfully written.

I thanked her for sharing, for honoring us with her story, for being brave enough to tell the truth. I promised her that by reading her piece she had already accomplished her goal of helping people, that I was certain she had already helped people in the room that night.

After that, hands shot up, one after another.

Stories of eating disorders, abuse, trauma, break-ups, loss of loved ones, survival, and how hard it was to show up against all odds to earn a degree were all told in the room that night.

Chills surged up and down my body again and again during the closing circle as each student shared what they were taking with them from their writing experience.

I thought I was the only one.

I didn't know I wasn't alone.

I thought everyone else in here had their shit together.

Hearing everyone else's problems has given me perspective on my own.

I didn't know writing could be like this. Maybe I'll try it again.

CREATIVE VS DESTRUCTIVE RISKS

One of my writing students and I did a barter. I'd give her a class and she'd come do to me one of the many things she was in training to do — Kundalini yoga, voodoo, deep tissue massage, sound therapy, cupping. On the day she aligned my chakras as I lay on a yoga mat next to the cat food bowls, her pendulum swung most wildly between my pubic bone and belly.

"Ah," she said. "This is where all of your energy is stored. The sacral chakra holds creativity, addiction, and sex."

What else is there? I wondered. Those were the three main things that existed in life, weren't they?

The trick, she told me, is channeling all of the energy used in addiction for creativity instead. I had arrived at this conclusion a thousand times myself but it felt profound hearing it from her as an accepted spiritual axiom.

My personal mission has been to transform my propensity for taking self-destructive risks into taking creative risks. To take the desire to feel alive by doing dangerous, crazy, or addictive things into a desire to create, to tap into the same energy stream, the same fire, and use it to warm rather than burn everything to the ground.

When I was 22 and a stewardess on a cruise ship in Alaska, the captain of the fleet said to me "Valley, beautiful women have the power to create or destroy. Be careful which one you choose." I've always remembered what he said to me in that moment in time, but I have to disagree. Everyone has the power to create or destroy and we must all be careful which one we choose. Power isn't in the exclusive domain of beauty.

As creative people, or people learning how to tap into our creativity, we are accessing a life force as potent, as life-giving, or as deadly as electricity or fire.

I used to feel like I was only connected to that live hot wire when I was drinking, hitchhiking, or going home with complete strangers.

Now I know I can connect to and access that same power by writing, exposing my stories and truths, by sharing in community. In the end it's so much more effective, more powerful and life giving. I remember my acts of creation the next day and no one gets hurt.

THE GREATER THE FEAR

Often, when someone is terrified of the writing process, I tell them what I believe to be true: the greater the fear we have, the greater the benefit we receive. I believe that when we write towards and through what frightens us the most, the more physical the emotion, the more profound the healing benefit we receive.

Apparently, this is the method my therapist uses too. Yesterday, our planned topic of discussion was how to keep myself from self-sabotaging, how not to avert oncoming happiness. How to embrace it instead. But it wasn't an intellectual or philosophical discussion that ensued. Instead she asked me to bring to mind a memory that made me cringe, a memory that caused an instinctive reflex to shut down.

This was easy. Ending up with my boyfriend's dad, I told her. Images from those weeks with him had been circling through the theatre of my mind making me want to gag each and every time.

"Good," she said. "Now what phrase do you relate to most?" And she handed me a piece of paper with about 50 phrases sorted by category. *I am bad. I am unworthy. I am afraid. I am broken.* "All of them," I said. "I can't possibly choose." "Okay," she said, taking the paper away. "Over-stimulation. Just concentrate on an image from that time and the feeling that comes with it."

As I closed my eyes, I could see the young girl with the old man, her desire to self-sacrifice, to inflict harm for the bad things she had done. I let the feelings of revulsion and harm pulse through my stomach and chest as my therapist encouraged and soothed me.

"Good work," she said when the session was done. And it was. There was no way to reach for happiness, to encourage wholeness, without first revisiting and repairing the damage that was done. The further we are willing to go into the depths of our stories and our lives, the more of our selves and stories we will be able to reclaim.

HOW TO SURVIVE PUBLIC HUMILIATION

1. Wake up at a fancy hotel and put on a nice dress before venturing out into your day. You have a better chance of surviving public humiliation if you are wearing actual clothes.

2. Feel really confident and happy when you sit down at a table with microphones and other panelists in front of a huge room of friends and strangers because what's the worst that can happen if you've made it this far?

3. When prompted, bumble and stumble your way through a pitch of the story of your life to a fellow panelist who happens to be the founding editor of a massively popular, well-renowned magazine.

4. Feel yourself flush beet red as he turns to you and says something that sounds just like this: "That was the worst pitch ever I've heard in my life and I would never accept it in a million years." Try to breathe as the air is sucked out of the room.

5. Laugh into the microphone and say something like: "And that's why I would never pitch the story of my life to your magazine."

6. Try not to die for the remaining 15 minutes of the panel even though it feels just like 15 lifetimes.

7. Collect your things and pretend your guts aren't exploding inside of your body. Say "FINE!" when a student asks you how you are and then fall apart when she asks you how you REALLY are.

8. Spend the next hour sobbing on a bench in the back of the conference and smile through your tears and snot when the security guards ask if you're okay. Drag up every mean, cruel, divisive thing anyone has ever said to you and replay it like shame porn on repeat.

9. Write an imaginary response to Mr. Man in your head peppered with the words *fuck* and *you* and *asshole* and then pray for him and pray for yourself and pray for all people everywhere who aren't caught gently when they stumble and fall and land on their face.

10. Spend the next three days asking people you love to remind you of what you once knew. That you are worthwhile and lovable, that one comment in one minute on one stage in one microphone does not define or lessen or negate what you have to give and say and do.

11. Keep writing. Keep crying. Clamp your heart open. Write the fuck out of what you have to write. Transform your shame into the fuel you need to keep going.

ADULT WOMAN

Driving home after class a few days ago, my mind flipped through my Rolodex of addictions wondering which I could pick to ease the empty feeling clawing at my chest from the inside out. Miraculously, instead of driving to a bar or to Target, I called my sponsor. Bless her heart, she said what she always says: "I know exactly how you feel." When her parents were battling sickness, dementia, cancer, and death her abandonment issues were triggered, too.

Until she said it I had no idea that's what it was. My eyes pricked with the sting of recognition.

"What have you done in the past when you felt this way?" she asked.

"Gotten drunk, bought cigarettes or weed, gone home with strange men in bars," I told her.

She laughed and then paused. "That's not exactly what I meant," she said. "What healthy things have you done when you've felt this way?"

"Oh," I said. "Cried, written, prayed, made calls, blah blah blah blah. It's just not as fun or as fast though, is it?"

She recommended I go home and listen to a yoga nidra in bed under piles of blankets and cats and anything else to help create that feeling of the safety and security of being held in a tight warm hug. When I followed her directions, the tears came in full and so did the complete and utter surrender to the release of sleep. When I got up an hour later I was ready to face the day, or at least start cooking.

I baked a spice cake slathered with vanilla icing, two sausage and broccoli quiches, and curry-roasted cauliflower to bring out to my dad and stepmother's house in the country, wedged between acres of farmland, lakes, and the brightly lit roller coasters and Ferris wheels of the State Fair like a mystical magical land of country and carnies. My dad moved 15 times before I turned 18 but has lived here ever since. 25 years. It's my home away from home.

Mary's hair is growing back in and her face glows with an inner light normally reserved for children or saints but the catheter is still inserted in her lung to drain the fluid and the cancer seems back to stay. Dad's tremors are increasing and the numbers of small animals scurrying about everywhere, all the time, inside the house and out are not growing smaller. Sometimes his hallucinations are big, sometimes small, always present. Cancer and Lewy Body Dementia could not have visited a more special, loving couple. For the last couple of years since each received their diagnosis, my heart has been in stages of breaking, healing, and re-breaking all over again.

After dinner, which tasted extraordinarily delicious thanks to the deep pleasure in providing nourishment as a tangible manifestation of love, I took a deep breath and suggested it was time to set a date to talk about their wills. "The ruby red pitcher that belonged to your Grandma Billie should be yours," Mary said. I thanked her and then with a series of awkward, false starts explained that division of objects and property was not exactly the conversation I had in mind. Rather, I need to know what happens to one if the other dies. Who wants a DNR? Will it be me making these decisions if the other isn't able? What happens to their bodies when they no longer contain breath?

In two weeks I will return with my laptop to write their answers down. "But how will we get a hard copy if it's on your computer?" my dad asked, technology a distant planet to him now. "Don't worry, I can print it out, Dad," I assured him, feeling all of those little internal gears and gadgets creating a capable adult woman inside of me begin to snap into place, ready to rise to the occasions that are required of me, heart, mind, body, and soul. I still need to comfort the helpless, terrified child inside, the one who doesn't want her parents to ever leave or change or go anywhere or die, but she can't be the one running the show. I have to take her hand and hold it so she doesn't take over.

SIGNED, SEALED, AND DELIVERED

The year I turned 21 and my mother turned 50, she held a Maiden-Crone ceremony for us in her backyard. All of my godmothers and adopted aunties chanted and prayed for us in a circle while my neighbor Frank watched open-mouthed from his back stoop.

My mother introduced me to all of her friends with short hair and flannel shirts the year she thought I was a lesbian.

She encouraged me to apply for a memoir-writing workshop with my idol, Madeleine L'Engle, even though I was too young. And because of her, I got in.

My mother sold her paintings so she could visit me in Florence and was loving and kind even though I went out drinking at night and cried my way through our mornings.

My mother read all of the books I read in elementary school so we could talk about them. We had no television. We made Shrinky Dinks and paintings and clay pots instead.

My mother drove me around the country in her Dodge minivan, camping along the way to conventions, peeing in buckets in our tents, navigating with books of triptychs from AAA.

My mother had thyroid cancer when I was three and when she went to the hospital for surgery I threatened to take all of my drawings down off of the walls I was so angry that she was gone.

When I left for college she gave me a framed colored pencil drawing she'd made of a woman standing in front of a row of produce holding a long green phallus in her hand. "Vegetables are good for you," the caption read.

She had ovarian cancer after I got married and then a fibroid tumor so big she spent a month in the hospital. She was always stubbornly determined to cure herself through raw foods, vegan juices, and the sheer grit of determination.

My mother and I fought like feral dogs, yelling and screaming and crying and calling each other names but we always made up in the end. She taught me how.

Once at a poetry reading when I was a teenager she looked at me across the room and said into the microphone, "All I did was open my legs twice and look at what I got."

**

My father taught me how to strike a match and how to build a fire. He taught me how to carve bows and arrows from still green and pliable wood, how to roll up in a sleeping bag to stay warm on a frigid night, how to hold onto the rails in the back of a pick up truck so you won't bounce out flying down a mountain.

My dad told me my fingers were so nimble I could be a surgeon. He told me I was smarter than he'd ever been. He made me feel special, intelligent, beloved.

My dad taught me to love the feeling of a canoe in a river, how to pick blueberries gone wild in a storm of brambles, and which trees have been gnawed on by beavers.

My dad shared with me his favorite records, books, and movies — *Harold and Maude*, Bob Dylan, *Gallipoli*, Bob Marley, *The Hotel New Hampshire*, Leonard Cohen, Bruce Cockburn, *The Days Run Away Like Wild Horses Over the Hills*, *Sherman's March*, Tom Waits, *My Dinner with Andre*. He helped me love them all with the same wide and deep and awestruck love that he did.

My dad took me furniture hunting through alleys and rock skipping across the river. We ate decadent, delicious food with our fingers. Every day with my dad was a party I never wanted to end and mourned with my whole heart every time it did.

When my dad started miscalculating, mis-cutting, and misfiring, bizarre mistakes for a master carpenter whose clients called him The Professor, who built gorgeous houses and gazebos and rocking chairs and shelves and sculptures out of wood, he started going in for tests, confounding even the smartest of doctors.

Those days and months when he saw fat redneck families with lobster claws invading his house, Confederate soldiers riding across the lawn on horseback, black men lynched from his front yard trees, those were the days I spent with him like he was my child.

**

Yesterday I saw my therapist for the first time in months. She took me back to that place where the arrow pierced through my chest, in one side and out the other. She asked what it felt like when my dad wasn't there and I fought so hard with my mom, what it will be like when they are gone. She used the word dead. "What will it be like?" she asked and I refused to answer the question.

"Does Adult Valley know how much she is loved?" she asked, and the tears came again, this time in the knowing, and that was where it hurt the most. The presence of so much love was more painful, more raw than the absence.

"I don't think their love for you was ever in doubt," my therapist said. "I think that's signed, sealed, and delivered." And I let that knowledge burn, sear straight through.

CHAPTER 7

Writing God

WRITING RELIGION

I have found writing and sharing our writing in community to be a form of worship — one that welcomes atheists and Jews, Catholics and Protestants, Buddhists, Muslims, Pagans, agnostics, priests, and bartenders alike.

There is a language that describes the human condition unfolding in each of us as universal as music. A language where we are stripped of exterior labels and identities and the songs of our hearts and souls and guts spill forth.

Once a pastor told me she went to church to work but she came to writing class to worship.

In our writing we can address our higher powers or our higher selves. We can address God or Buddha or Jesus or the divine goddess or nature. We can tap into the stream of the universe that feeds us, whether it stems from chaos, from quiet, from heaven and peace, or from our own version of hell.

Writing about my relationship with God, prayer, spirituality, and belief is some of the most intimate, the most vulnerable writing I do. Rarely do I write directly about my version of God but just as rarely is my writing devoid of her completely. What I believe is the fuel that pushes my pen.

We don't have to be religious or even spiritual to feel the connection that writing in a safe community can provide. We just have to be human enough to show up and be who we are — no small task in the world outside.

One minister who took my class said he kept coming back because it brought him comfort to see how screwed up we all are and how we're all working on healing in our own different ways.

The classes I've taught to deacons at a church and yoga teachers in training have been moving, beautiful and deep. They had everything to do with our shared humanity and little to do with the particular altar where we bend our knee.

If we can sit in a room and say out loud what's truly happening beneath our outside personas and costumes and roles and masks as best we can, that's a good way to honor the sacred for me.

What memories and experiences are sacred to you? How do you honor them?

WRITING MEDITATION

When I first tried to meditate, I could not make it through ten minutes without literally finding myself all the way across the room doing something else entirely. I have never been good at being still or being alone or allowing my thoughts to pass by like ripples on a sun-dappled stream. While it's clear meditation is something we practice rather than perfect, it sure didn't seem like the stampede in my mind was going anywhere at all.

Because so many spiritual traditions advocate meditation, I've kept trying despite so many ill-fated attempts. I've found that guided or walking meditations are more successful for me than silent ones. But perhaps the most effective form I've found is the written meditation, allowing the wild beasts of my mind to funnel through my pen, emerging as words moving across the page.

Many spiritual traditions also encourage us to stay in the present moment, to be here now, to savor the gifts of the day. Beginning with the words "Right Now I Am" is a powerful way to launch a written meditation.

We can write with intention, slowing our hand and the pace of our thoughts. We can meditate on a mantra or a prayer or a theme or simply follow what's already there waiting to come out all on its own. In this case, the process of writing holds more healing properties than the product. Written meditations are about the act of slowing down, going within, and listening deeply to our innermost selves, not about creating a piece for critique or publication.

They say prayer is talking to God and meditation is listening. Written meditation is a way of creating the space to listen, opening the doors for our higher powers or higher selves or still small voices within to enter and walk through.

If I can manage to eat a meal or wash the dishes in a meditative state, I can certainly focus quietly on the page, alone with my words, and the space that forms in between.

DEAR GOD...

My mom says the first night she learned to pray she imagined a hot guy named Judah holding her in his arms. I was two years old and when I woke up the next morning I said, "Mommy, my angels were with me last night." It was the same year my dad left, her mom died, and she got sober. The older women in AA had taught my mom how to talk to God earlier that day.

Ever since, my mom has loved to pray. Every entry in the many spiral-bound journals beside her bed begin with "Dear God..." She prayed before bed, in our car, before we left the house. At meals, even the ones we ate on the floor when the dining room table was too crowded to clear. When we passed an ambulance or a fire truck. My mom turned to prayer as often as she turned to cursing. I learned *God, fuck, shit, damn,* and *angels watch over me* pretty much all at once. And therein lies the spiritual life of the recovering alcoholic. I've never disowned my mother's God like lots of people have to do. I've adopted him, or maybe he's adopted me. He is loving, kind, and beautiful. He is warm and full of grace. He cares about the intimate, innermost details of me and has a wicked sense of humor. He is also a he-she-mother-father-God encapsulating all and none of the genders and polarities within the grasp of my understanding.

Now I find myself praying all the time. I have a kind of shorthand special code language with God. We talk about big and little things, magic, parking spots, death, plumbing, missing cats, heartache, life's meaning, grief, addiction, and what I should make to eat next.

God is teaching me to love me, to stop beating up, chastising, over-expecting, demanding and controlling me. I don't pray on my knees or in church but I keep a running commentary with God, like a long text thread with a funny, wise, and responsive friend. God can take my ugly, my messy, my nasty and feral and wild just as well as the good and sparkly parts of me. Sometimes I write prayers to God in my journal, pleas, notes, memos, wish lists, and reminders, like I remember my mom used to do. They're not fancy or formal but God doesn't seem to care. Writing prayer is a way of communicating who I am and what I need right now, not who anyone else thinks I should be.

WRITING PRAYER

Writing our prayers is a practical way to perform a holy act. It's a way to communicate directly with our definition of the divine. Writing down what we hope for, what terrifies us, our fears and our longing keeps those feelings from staying trapped as thoughts in our minds. The physical act of communication with our versions of God—in the form of nature, the universe, or a deity—helps give form to our side of the conversation.

Writing our prayers is a way to take our turmoil, our blessings, our pleases and thank yous and give them focus, direction, and meaning. My written prayers contain both the sacred and the profane. They encompass the big and the little. My prayers are vulnerable, personal, and often nonsensical. That's okay. The God I believe in does not judge grammar or content. The God I believe in might know my prayers before I write them down but finding the language to clarify what's happening in my spirit helps me.

I keep a notebook in my window seat with my meditation books and candles. After I've sat down and written a prayer to God I feel more connected and more clear. I might plead and beg, rant or rave. I often write prayers about my writing life, asking to be given direction and purpose. It's easier for me to let go of the things on my mind when I know they are safely protected somewhere.

We do not have to share our prayers with anyone, but it might be useful for us to look back on them ourselves from time to time. What were we able to let go of? What was answered or heard? What are we still working through that we might need to add to our prayers again?

THE REAL JOURNEYS

The first time I pray alone, I am hugging a guard rail on the side of the road, trucks and bald eagles roaring past, as I walk into Juneau, Alaska from the trailer park where I'm staying on the outskirts of town. The owner of the trailer has made it quite clear I am not welcome to stay much longer in her trailer for free but my wallet has been stolen from a bar in Olympia, I can't stop crying, and I have 32 cents to my name. In the depths of the Last Frontier, as far across the country as I can get from my home, feeling scared and alone, I have to figure out how to make it on my own. "Dear God, please help me find a fucking job," I pray.

At the first establishment I enter, I am hired as a stewardess on a cruise ship leaving the very next day. Gino, the captain of the fleet, tells me four things in his office overlooking the rooftops of the beautiful, frozen town. First, that I will have to take a Coast Guard-issued drug test before I am sanctioned to sail. A drug test that, if failed to pass, will result in immediate termination and removal from the ship. Second, that if a certain person were afraid they would fail a certain drug test, that person could buy a certain tea from a certain health food store across a certain town. He points out the window at a rooftop and I squint to see. Third, Gino says he has an old leather-bound edition of *Gulliver's Travels*, the very book I am reading, and if I stay until the end of the season he will give it to me. Last, he tells me that he thinks he's falling in love with me. "Women like you are so brave," he says, and at 22, the thing that surprises me most is that he calls me a woman.

I say the second prayer I remember saying on my walk to the health food store across town. And God answers my prayer yet again, but not in the ways I expect. Yes, I pass the drug test, but it's also on this boat that I get sober, despite my best intentions to remain permanently drunk. In the interest of passenger safety, it is against Coast Guard regulation for crew to drink during the season. And though I sneak off the boat into dark seedy bars to knock back shots of liquor or wine or beer several times during the summer to escape the impossible blaring pain of reality, I am never once able to get drunk again.

When I call my mother from a payphone on the dock in Juneau to tell her that I want to quit, she says, "Valley, whatever you do, do not get off that ship." My boyfriend, she tells me, has found out about his dad and me, about our two weeks together without him that summer. My boyfriend tells her he's either going to kill himself or kill me. My mother begs me to not step foot on dry land. I agree.

And so while scrubbing heads and making beds, I watch whales breach every morning against impossibly brilliant sunrises. The Chief Steward lets me trade vacuuming duty in exchange for haiku. I write poems, letters, ballads, prayers, songs. I learn how to exist in a confined space with other people, how to ride a motorbike, how to dive off the stern of the ship, how to stay. I can't run away. In the middle of the sea, there is nowhere to run.

When the boat docks at the end of the summer I call my mother collect again. "I want to keep traveling," I tell her. "There's so much more I want to do and see." This time she asks me to come home. It's Yom Kippur. Her brother's getting married.

"The real journeys aren't out there," she tells me. "The real journeys are inside you." Inside me there are glaciers of frozen heartbreak, chunks of solid ice, torrents of grief and storm, but also whales and whispers and prayers. I know she's right. It's time to start a different journey. It's time to come home.

A CALLING TO WRITE

When I got sober and started working the steps in my recovery program, I was terrified to turn my life and my will over to a higher power as I understood him/her/it. I was convinced this new God would strip me of my sense of humor, my love of the underworld, and my desire to be a writer. In fact, I was convinced God would make me become a nun. And I knew I would be a horrible nun.

Fortunately, I shared this with a woman in the program who assured me that God did not want me to become a nun. In fact, she said, the desires in my heart were planted there by the very God I was so afraid of. God wanted for me what I most wanted for myself. To become completely me, to pursue my passions, to write my heart out. There were enough women in the convent already, she said.

A well-established author I knew told me she thought pursuing your passion was the most practical career path because it meant interviewing for jobs you were naturally good at. This was an enormous relief and over the years, as I've turned towards what I love to do most, writing and teaching, ways have opened up for me to continue doing them. Mysterious, beautiful, weird ways that must have been orchestrated by someone much craftier and smarter than me. Pursuing the path of a writer and self-employed writing teacher has involved a fair amount of uncertainty and ramen noodles. But I've never gone hungry — in stomach or spirit.

Of course, you absolutely do not have to quit your day job in order to write. You do not have to drop out of your own life to live in a cabin in the woods with a notebook and a pen. Writing can be done anywhere, complementing any lifestyle. If you feel the calling to write, you can answer that call no matter what else is happening in your life.

BREATH OF FIRE

When I enter yoga class I instinctively move as far away from the handsome bearded man as possible, finding myself unfortunately positioned in front of the big mirrors facing the rest of the class instead. Calm down, I remind myself. This is for you. And I unroll my mat, desperate to connect my mind with my body. These days desperate can also mean uncomfortable. 1 or 99 percent, doesn't matter. I am the Princess and the Pea. Small splinters are great arrows.

The focus of the class is breathing which I have noticed in other yoga classes lately I don't know how to do. I often find myself gasping — not because I'm winded but because the air has displaced itself and I have to chase after it, gulp it down before it disappears.

The yoga instructor leads us through Breath of Fire, Breath of Joy, deep stomach breaths, nose breaths, breaths where we look and feel like wild animals all caged up together in the same room. I am grateful for the opportunity to practice because it all feels pretty important. We move, too. I stretch and roll and reach and bend, telling myself I am re-entering my body, that it is a safe and okay place to be.

I only make the mortal error of looking in the mirror once and then gently force myself to be kind to the girl staring back. Everyone else is just here with me, not worse or better. I am not on display, I am practicing introducing my mind to my body like everyone else.

The instructor apologizes for a short savasana but I think all the breathing brings it home fast. You were not a mistake, I hear from somewhere deep inside as soon as I close my eyes. Hot tears spilled over and I can see and feel and hear the little girl whose parents loved her but could not figure out how to love each other. The little girl who carried this feeling without words to frame it: if my mother and father's marriage wasn't meant to be, what of anything that came out of it?

I don't have to force myself to be kind to the girl who asks these questions. My love for her comes out hot and steady, like breath.

UPPER WORLD

This morning I had a larger block of time than usual for meditation so I decided to try a shamanic journey to the Upper World. It was 23 minutes long and required me to make the room as dark as possible so I put a facemask over my eyes. Another Upper World journeyer had left a bitter and nasty review about his shamanic journey—or lack thereof—and I wanted to see if it would be the same big fat dud for me or if I'd meet my spirit guides and have my questions answered as promised in the promo.

What I found in the rattle and the drum and the woman's voice giving guided visual suggestions was even more astonishing. As we climbed a rainbow through the clouds, I felt a mirror, an echo, of the journeys John Hunter, my gifted and talented class SPACE teacher, took us on when we met every week in the basement of my haunted elementary school. The rainbow was a bridge and a bow, leading me up from the bottom.

I also saw Jesus on my shamanic journey, the version my mother created for me as a child. A bearded, dark-skinned man with a big lap you could crawl into when you were sad or tired. The answers I got from both John Hunter and Jesus were perhaps unsurprising to the enlightened but hit me hard. Forget about success, they said. Whether I publish my next book or not doesn't matter. What matters is learning how to fully occupy my body, my mind, my house, my family, my life. Living well is more important than writing well, a formula I've always had in reverse.

And the last couple of weeks have in fact been a testament to this. A new level of ownership and empowerment and joy in my own being has arisen—a level of content and happiness and serenity I'm almost uncomfortable with. I'm a chaos addict and a drama queen. What the hell am I supposed to do now? The other day I thought I hope I get so happy there's nothing left to write about at all. But life is the great equalizer and I know that everything that comes, comes to pass. Happiness, grief, clouds, rainbows, shamanic journeys, the times we want to write our stories like our life depends on it and the times we need to live to have something to write about at all.

SHIT LIST, WISH LIST, THANK YOU LIST

Since some time roughly between Jesus and Oprah, well-intentioned people the world over have been recommending that you write a "gratitude list," especially when the shit hits the fan. While it's true that a good gratitude list can change your perspective, shift your perception, and help you remember why life is worth living, I have found it hard to just sit down and arrive directly at gratitude in any real way, especially when it feels like the entire world has just ended, or at least been taken over by a fascist demagogue. So I've come up with a workaround. First I write a "Shit List," then I write a "Wish List," and THEN I write a "Thank You List." I find I can make room for gratitude after I've done some work clearing the way.

Find some paper and a pen or pencil. I recommend writing by hand because it's a more direct line to your heart and it's harder to check Facebook. Write "Shit List" at the top of the page and then let it rip. Don't worry about spelling, punctuation, or grammar while you're doing it. Don't even worry about forming complete sentences or making any kind of sense at all. This is YOUR shit list and you can put anything and everything you want on it, from the horrors in the world to the horrors of having to wash another sinkful of dishes (and everything in between). No one has to read it! This is just for you. Think of it as your personal exorcism. Your chance to vent, unload, confess and complain without having to apologize to anyone.

Once you are emptied out of all that is draining you right now, go to a clean page and write "Wish List." Here are your dreams for the world, for your friends, for your family, and for yourself. Here is the space to envision and imagine and create. Go wild. Create your own personal utopia. Why not?

At last you are ready for your Thank You List. What exists in the world, in your life, right now, exactly as it is, that you are grateful for? My mother once put it to me this way: imagine anything you don't write on your gratitude list might be taken away. That makes shit real, doesn't it? Do you have arms, legs, fresh food and water? Do you have someone to love whether it's a child, adult, or cat? Do you have clothing and shelter and a friend? Can you order pizza and have it delivered RIGHT TO YOUR DOOR? There's a lot to be grateful for right here and now. Give yourself a chance to remember that. It will give you renewed energy when there's work to be done.

CHAPTER 8

Write the Power

WRITE THE POWER

Telling the truth and healing our pain is a revolutionary and political act. Writing down what we believe and putting our writing into the world is an act of resistance. Telling our stories as survivors, as minorities, as women, as those in recovery or struggling with issues of mental health, illuminates the world's narrative. Using our privilege to support and uplift those whose voices are not heard is our birthright and our imperative.

We don't have to wait until we are perfect or enlightened or published or have a position of great power to add our voice to the political arena. We can heal ourselves and give back to the world in tandem.

We may need a writing class to help us find our voice, to help us discover our beliefs, how to articulate those beliefs and direct them out into the world in a way that can affect change. Or we may need a writing class to shut out the nonstop news of the world that inundates us every day. We may need the quiet time of a class to process what's going on within ourselves, while holding the ocean of the world at bay. Both of these choices are good and correct. We can use our voice to fight oppression and prejudice from without and examine and heal our own implicit bias within.

We can write letters to editors, senators, and back pages. We can discover what we think, what we believe, and what is within our reach to do. We can find quiet within the maelstrom of political chaos to figure out what is important to us, what we have to offer, and how we can best use our time in the service of the world.

What is the intersection of the political and the personal in your life? How would you write about the issues that matter the most to you?

WRITING THE RESISTANCE

The night that Donald Trump was elected president I dreamed I was trying to type the word "nightmare" but my fingers couldn't grasp onto the letters to spell the word. I dreamed the sentence "I haven't had enough trauma therapy for this," and when I rose to go to the bathroom I stepped barefoot in cat vomit. But finally waking in the morning was far worse. As I tried to fully process the news, weeping loudly in my bed, my son called from across the house. "Mom? You know that learning curve you showed me, with all the troughs and plateaus? America's in a learning curve right now. Half of America is just trying to catch up."

And then he asked if online petitions or paper petitions were more effective. Because surely the half of America that voted for Donald Trump didn't realize he'd been endorsed by the KKK. He wanted to let them know. I didn't have the heart to tell him I was pretty sure they already did.

Together my son and I frantically Googled "What to Tell Your Children" because I couldn't come up with any comforting words on my own. It felt to me like the earth had cracked open and would swallow us up. It felt like blood was running in the streets. That The End was near. That history would repeat itself, here in the Land of the Free.

"So will he have to start wearing a Star of David to school now?" my husband asked, giving words to the horror I felt in the deepest pit of my stomach, my soul. But not just for us, the Jews. For African-Americans and Hispanics and Muslims and the LGBTQ community. For women. For the men and boys who are married to and loved by and needed by and mothered by them.

That morning, getting dressed and driving to the Writing Room for my class felt like play-acting in a surreal alternate reality. I had done my very best in this election cycle to keep the names of particular political figures out of the classroom, to make it a safe place for everybody. This morning I told my class, "Fuck that. We need to process. We need to grieve. We need to be honest. We need to heal. Let it all out. Any way you need to."

And that's what we did. Not everyone in the room held the same opinions as me. One woman said she almost didn't come to class because she felt her position wouldn't be popular. I thanked her profusely for being brave and honest, for shining a light on another perspective, for telling her truth even though she was afraid. I believe in my deepest heart of hearts that being honest and listening deeply to each other will help us heal. And for me, that means speaking out and speaking up, showing up and not shutting down. Doing everything I can in my little circle of the world to make it a safe, loving, kind, nurturing, accepting place for everyone to be exactly who and what they are. To have every color skin, every sexuality, ability, class, income and religion or lack thereof. I will not be silent. I will not give in.

"What does it mean to join the resistance?" a friend asked me later that day.

"I don't know," I said. "But we're going to find out."

NAMES OF EXOTIC GODS AND CHILDREN

I knew I was pregnant for the first time when I found Hooker decomposing in the far pasture. I sat on a rock next to her corpse and cracked open the beer I'd stashed in my apron for the journey to find her body. Above us the sky threatened to split open, clouds gathering in their own dark herd. Hooker's rib cage looked like exposed rafter beams in a high-ceilinged barn. Surrounded by wildflowers and aspen trees I wept for the both of us. Big Will had taught me how to ride her, how to hold on tight and grip her enormous body with all of the power in my belly and thighs. She'd taught me it was possible to fly across fields and up mountains and through valleys. She taught me it was possible to be beautiful and strong and still surrender when it was time to die.

Big Will and I were engaged, or at least I wore his old wedding ring wrapped with tape so it would stay on my finger. We found a different cabin to sleep in each night—whichever wasn't occupied by guests at the time. Once, one of the wood stoves caught fire, with us inside the cabin. My denim and velvet dress and extra bra had burned to ash. The only thing left of our pile of clothing was his silver belt buckle which he saved like a trophy.

I loved him but he still couldn't spell my name right and I didn't want to have his baby. I knew I wanted to be a mother, but not yet. I still had to drink and smoke and fuck my way across the country. I still had to grow up myself.

Big Will took me to Planned Parenthood on one of our days off to confirm what I already knew. "Congratulations!" beamed the nurse and I thought she must be talking to someone else, or crazy. This was not good news at all. In fact, I couldn't imagine anything worse. My idyllic cabin girl in the Wild West fantasy shattered around me, replaced by morning sickness, exhaustion, and nausea.

We scheduled an appointment to come back to the clinic, but in the meantime it was hunting season and getting colder. I saw less of the horses and more of the kitchen. I moved into Big Will's top bunk in the bunkhouse, dragging my few belongings behind me. He was a beast at 6'5" and there wasn't much space for me in his room full of dogs and men.

No more poker nights and singing around bonfires. No more galloping across fields or down the sides of mountains blanketed with wildflowers of every color with names like exotic gods or children.

In the parking lot, there were protesters everywhere. I hated them. How dare they make something so hard that much harder? I'd never really felt the need to wear armor but I wanted it now. To be shielded, invisible, invincible. To have the privacy of my own pain. There were a lot of forms to fill out and papers to sign. Big Will and I split the price 50–50 from our tips from the ranch, a big chunk of the money we'd planned to travel with when we were free. I scanned a list of horrible potentials as I signed my name. Bleeding, cramping, fatigue, and then the worst of all: continued pregnancy. I thought that possible outcome worse than the possibility listed next: death.

I hyperventilated on the table with the doctor's hands and heavy metal tools crammed into my body. "Keep looking at my beautiful face," the nurse said again and again, squeezing my hand as I tried to breathe, pain and fear and blinding lights tight and clamping down on the black hole between my legs. Finally it was over and somehow they sat me up and put me back together as best they could. As Big Will pulled out of the parking lot I mouthed *fuck you* to the protesters shouting in our wake, but the truth was, I didn't know who I hated more. Me or him or them.

We returned to the ranch up Coffee Pot Road leaving government land behind, zigzagging up the bumpy, impossibly deep grooves in the earth. I returned to the kitchen and the wringer-washer washing machine and the dishes and laundry as best I could. But I didn't feel like singing along to the country songs on our little FM radio anymore. On my afternoon break, instead of exploring or hiking or writing, I wrapped myself in quilts and curled up like a baby.

It was one week later that I got a call from my mother. The singular phone on the ranch was in a little alcove next to the kitchen and rarely worked. Phone calls were uncommon, if not unheard of. My mother's voice coming through the crackling static on the other end of the phone reached through the line and homesickness ached through my bones. "Valley!" my mom shouted. "The clinic's been trying to reach you. They couldn't get through."

I'd given my mom's number as my emergency contact. I'd gotten into the habit of living places one could not call.

"Oh?" I yelled back. The wranglers were starting to mill about, gathering for dinner. I tried to pretend I was alone in the room. "The procedure didn't work," I heard my mother's voice say. The news bounced off and then thunked into my belly like a heavy stone. There was still a baby alive inside of me. "Mom," I said. "I want to come home."

She sent me a plane ticket and by the next week I had packed up my canvas Army Navy bag and was gone. It was too much to say goodbye to those mountains, to that valley, to the cabins and the lodge and Hooker and the horses and the flowers and my fiancé and all of the other wranglers I'd grown not to like, but to love. I said this lie: see you soon, and returned to the clinic before getting on the plane so they could redo the job they had failed at before. I cried the whole plane ride home, suspended in the sky above our country, freed from the cluster of molecules, the magical cells, the holy organism in my body that had tried so hard to hang on.

My mother picked me up from the airport and moved me into her queen-sized bed back home. I was bleeding and cramping and full of rage and sorrow and grief. Pain took hold of my guts and squeezed hard like those cold metal clamps were still there, as if they always would be.

The Hydrocodone and Valium did not take away the pain but wrapped it in a flimsy layer of gauze. I lay in the fetal position twisted up in blankets on my mother's bed for a week as she nursed me back to health with broth and tea and love. Sometimes I still turn over names for the child that could have been, but I never come up with one that is good.

CHOICE

After the election I switched my primary care to Planned Parenthood to show my support for their practice through both my physical presence and my insurance dollars. It felt like a powerful and profoundly good idea until several hours before my appointment Monday morning when I woke up heart pounding in my chest, tears streaming down my cheeks. The last time I'd been to a Planned Parenthood was nearly 20 years ago in Denver, Colorado.

I'd hyperventilated on the table as the nurse tried to regulate my breathing, asking me again and again to keep my eyes trained on her beautiful face. I'd bled, cramped, and cried for days in my narrow bunk at the lodge in the Flat Tops Wilderness Area where I was a cabin girl. And then, of all horrible things, I'd found out that the procedure hadn't been successful and that they'd have to do it again. After the second time, instead of going back to finish hunting season, my mom booked me a plane ticket home.

Despite the pain and grief of that experience, it is the experience that allowed me to have the life I have today. To become a mother when I was ready to become a mother, not when I was still young and wild and had so much growing up left to do. Almost exactly a year later I got sober and met the man who would become my husband and a wonderful, loving father. I have become a teacher and a writer because I have had the space and time to do so at my own pace. Choosing my own path has not just been a part of my life, it has created the life I have.

Before the appointment on Monday morning, I took a long cold walk through my neighborhood with a friend who reminded me that I had choices then and that I have choices now. That I could go and then leave if I wanted to. That I didn't have to do anything I wasn't comfortable doing. And that I didn't have to do any of it alone. This reminder was exactly what I needed. I waited in the waiting room like an adult woman and had my routine exam like an adult woman too. The doctors, nurses, and administrators were kind, smiling, warm, friendly, professional, and patient. I thanked them and they all smiled and said they appreciated it, especially on a Monday morning.

And then I allowed myself the luxury of spending the rest of the day drinking tea and reading my book in bed. Profoundly and overwhelmingly grateful that I had the ability, the grace, and the choice to do what was best for me. What's best for me moving forward is doing everything I can to ensure other girls and women have choices, too.

WRITING ABOUT RACE

I am white. I am Jewish. My mother has been asked if she's Chinese, Mexican, a Gypsy. I tan well, but there's no denying the whiteness of my skin, the intactness of my privilege, the impossibility of understanding even a fraction of what it means or how it feels to experience racism against people of color in America. Which is why I continued to ignore the persistent interior call I felt to lead a writing workshop about race in Richmond.

And then I couldn't get the face of *Richmond Magazine* journalist Samantha Willis out of my head. We'd been friends on Facebook for years but had never met in person. Finally, I sent her a message proposing we lead a writing workshop on race together. She wrote back almost immediately explaining she was in the middle of an email to me proposing the exact same thing. And not only that, she was in the beginning stages of putting together a three-part series called *#UnmaskingRVA* to talk specifically about issues of race in Richmond.

Our ideas for the structure of our workshop came together quickly. Within two days of posting, it filled — with a waiting list. Samantha and I showed up that Tuesday night in December wearing the exact same outfit: black pants and red sweaters, only my jewelry was silver, hers gold. When the room filled to capacity, half of the writers were white, half black. I was relieved but also terrified. I believed with all my heart in the power of writing to bring people together, to unite and to heal but how could I possibly be qualified to facilitate conversation around a topic I could never fully understand?

Sam gave her first prompt: "When was the first time in your life you realized race was an issue?" Everyone wrote and then read personal experiences from their childhoods directly connected to the biggest, ugliest tragedy of our nation: systemic racism, subtle and overt. I gave feedback about the writing; Sam responded to the specific issues of race. The stories were moving, revelatory, revealing, heartbreaking, and profound. But when it was suggested I read my piece too, I deflected.

At last I realized I had to read. It wasn't fair to ask others to do what I myself would not. I had to face the terrifying vulnerability of exposing a time in my life of deep shame and early heartbreak.

When I was in first or second grade at my predominantly African-American elementary school in the East End, a few of the kids accused me of starting slavery. Some of the kids threatened to beat me upside the head. Other kids shared their snacks with me at lunch, stood with me against the brick wall of the playground, were kind and generous and loving but I was scared and lonely much of the time. In other words, we were kids left to the jungle of the schoolyard, acting out in various ways what we knew. For decades, the old guilt and shame mixed with an intense longing to be loved and accepted by brown people and black people, by my classmates, had lodged itself in my heart like a silent thorn.

My story was lovingly and compassionately received by the group. My brief experience as other accepted without judgment or scorn. Reading my work out loud helped extract an ancient splinter. The openness and deep sharing from everyone else around the table that night as we continued to write and read and talk and share was a precious gift. At the end of the night others expressed their gratitude for the level of honesty and openness we achieved, but I can only hope others received a fraction of what I did. I know there are a million more conversations to be had, countless stories to be written, ancient, deep wounds to be healed. But I also know none of that will happen if we let silence or fear win. If we don't begin.

When were you first aware that race was an issue? How have issues of race impacted you and your life?

WHY I'M NOT BREAKING UP WITH THE WORLD JUST YET

The last couple of weeks I have wanted to break up with the world, or at least file a pretty heavy-duty restraining order. Watching all manner of bigotry and hate crimes spike like fever everywhere I turn has gutted me.

But along with all the horror washed up on our shore, some pretty fucking beautiful buried treasure has surfaced, too. God or the Universe or George or Martha or whoever is in charge up there has been sending me ambassadors of humanity, angels dressed as strangers perhaps so I won't divorce all of humankind and go live in a hole just yet. I haven't felt such a deep connection with people I don't know since that cross-country Greyhound ride in the mid-90s. (Dorothea, if you haven't found the purple people flying outside your window yet, I hope they found you.)

When I told my checkout clerk at Target I was losing it, she came around her aisle to hug me. "I'm black and I'm a lesbian," she said. "But we're in this thing together." I accepted her comfort and was grateful for the human connection of such a warm hug.

When I emailed a local journalist I've admired for years because I couldn't get her face out of my head, proposing we lead a workshop together, she wrote back seconds later, "I was just writing the exact same thing to you." At my first eye exam in eight years (you have to be able to see clearly if you want to fight in the resistance) my new optometrist told me all of his deep and beautiful feelings and theories and beliefs about writing while commanding my left eye to follow his index finger. On a cold, dreary day this week, the UPS man slowed down to tell me he'd never forget my son chasing his truck to give him a cold glass of lemonade on a hot summer day. And all kinds of beautiful people showed up at the Speak Your Truth Writing Workshop at the Presbyterian Church in Northside hungry to share, express, work, and heal. People, who, just a few weeks before, would not have all been in the same room together.

So. We may still need body armor to shield ourselves from falling debris, but we need crowbars to keep our hearts pried open, too. I'm not breaking up with the world just yet. There are more ambassadors for humanity I want to meet, more stories I want to hear.

WRITING WARRIOR

We are all warriors when we show up to the page with the intention of writing something true. We may be in the middle of our own personal battles, about to set out, or just back from the war. We may feel energized and fresh or scarred and battle weary, but our mission is to lay down our weapons in order to write from a place that is vulnerable and honest and true.

Warriors have not led pristine or easy lives. They have seen destruction and bloodshed. They are fierce defenders of what they believe and hold to be true. They have been through tests and trials, training and combat. The warrior, just by being alive, has won. The warrior has a story to tell. Not about how perfect life was, but about how she survived, what was lost, and what was hard-won. The warrior does not use her weapons against herself. She uses them to protect what she wants to create and what she loves the most.

The warrior must protect her fortress. She can't allow the enemy in. She knows when to keep her armor on and when it's best to take it off. She does not apologize for her story, for everything it took to arrive at the page. She honors it, she defends it, she fights for its right to exist on its own. She does not allow comparison, judgment, or apology to rule the day. She's a fierce defender of her right to exist, to take up space, to be.

Whether your war has been out in the world, within your body or mind, you have a story to tell that is yours, and yours alone.

WARRIOR TRAINING

I want to thank the people who have hurt me the most, who have made me question my worth as a woman, who have provoked, undervalued, and betrayed me. They were part of my warrior training.

I want to thank the women who have wanted and needed and demanded too much. The men who have given too little. They were part of my warrior training.

I want to thank the people I let in who I shouldn't have, the over-steppers, the boundary-pushers. They have been part of my warrior training.

I want to thank those who don't approve, won't flatter, reciprocate, or perform. They have forced me into warrior training.

I want to thank the poverty and food stamps, insecurity, uncertainty, years of rocky and treacherous ground. That was part of my warrior training.

I want to thank the days that did not turn out as I expected, the times I did not get what I wanted, rejection, guilt, and shame. That's all been part of my warrior training.

I want to thank the people I love who are dying, people who are sick, who feel that they are broken. They have given me so much in my warrior training.

I want to thank my friends and sisters, mothers and aunties, crones, maidens, and wise women, leaders and teachers and prophets and visionaries and artists and writers near and far who have led the way for warrior training.

I want to thank my own fear, my own rage, my uncertainty and silence. The voice that has risen, is rising. There is so much work to be done. I am, we are, warriors in training.

CHAPTER 9

Writing the Ceasefire

CEASEFIRE

When we surrender our weapons and call a ceasefire, we stop fighting, primarily ourselves. We pour our time and energy and spirit into what's working instead of battling what's not. We concentrate on our strength, rather than expending all our energy battling our demons, trying to win a battle we are bound to lose.

They say that if a wolf is chasing you, don't run. Stand still and turn your back. You cannot outrun the wolf. In writing we must continually redirect our energy so that we don't waste it running away from what frightens us most.

When we stop and get quiet long enough to write we allow our pain and our past and our feelings to catch up with us, to pass through us. And this is where the raw stuff of our lives is alchemically transformed into something else. Our histories, our survival maps, our memoirs, our art. When we surrender, we do not have to give up our beliefs, convictions, values, our self-protection or preservation. When we stop fighting the chaos of the world and ourselves, when we finally surrender, we are empowered to use our energy and our voice for healing that extends inward towards ourselves and outwards into the world.

We do not need more armed militias, more combat zones, more violence. We need more compassion, empathy, and understanding. We need to listen to each other and we need our stories to be heard. I have screamed, slammed doors, and thrown hard objects against walls, but I have effected a lot more change in my own family by listening, asking questions, and voicing my needs. I've spent plenty of time using a voice so loud no one could hear what it was I had to say.

The pen, they say, is mightier than the sword. If we are able to articulate our beliefs, speak our convictions, and write down what we are most passionate about, we can wield our stories and our voices to create powerful change within ourselves and the world.

WHAT DO I WRITE ABOUT NOW?

The family drama feels like it's past the most dangerous beasts in the jungle (at least the ones we already know, for this moment, today, right now).

When I do the internal body scan, all of my immediate family members are in the right place. My heart is in the heart cavity, lungs beneath the rib cage, brain nestled in the head, stomach and guts anchoring the whole thing together from the seat of their own wild ocean.

Husband and son are limbs and skin and bone and blood. No unnecessary appendages hanging on, no painful amputations either.

The body of my life is not in a state of emergency and I don't know how to write about that. How do you write about things going well?

I know how to write about my own grief and longing and chaos, from the place of shame and humiliation, from fear and the inner rings of hell. But when all the clothes are hung up in the closets, the bodies are accounted for and I feel like making dinner for the people I love, what is left then?

Should I start reporting the pain and hurt of other people's lives? Writers who are the mouthpiece for the suffering of others are so brave and so noble but I'm afraid I'll never resurface from those waters, never recover.

Every grief, dysfunction, and shred of my own suffering quivers in the fire of my first manuscript waiting for my edits swaddled like a baby or a bomb in the corner of my room and I'm afraid to even peek in its general direction lest it cry or explode.

Can I just enjoy the simplicity of life for a moment when things are going well? Am I allowed to? Can I even stand it, or will I stir it all back up just because I can? The honest truth is I've been praying for peace but at its arrival it's like I've allowed a stranger through the front door who sits awkwardly on the couch in the living room.

A friend of mine had a professor who told the students in his creative writing class that they should never go to therapy. "You'll have nothing left to write about," he told them. But I disagree. I have to. Staying stuck in misery and darkness is not as interesting to read or write about as transformation, metamorphosis, or at long last finding light. I love it when my students share moments of grace and joy. Engagements, marriages, births, new puppies, new homes, recovery, progress, therapy, reunions, forgiveness, revelations, life. When we hear about other people's happiness we have a blueprint we can use to find our own.

WATER SEEKS ITS OWN LEVEL

I almost said to my husband, "Don't you know we're supposed to be together forever?" as we leaned against the radiator on the floor of a crowded AA meeting. I'd only known him for 30 days, we'd only spoken once or twice and luckily, I caught the words before they left my mouth, swallowed them back down, and asked him if he knew the time instead.

He was handsome and bright and I could feel a solid goodness deep within him. Though he was polite and reserved with me, the dreams I had about him made me feel I'd known him forever already and would end up knowing him longer than that. In one we ran a marathon together and at the end, as we flopped exhausted into the dirt beneath our feet, he offered me his hand to use as a pillow. In the other we sailed around the world on a small swift ship.

We had a lot of near misses where he avoided me or I avoided him. I was reading books on how to date while trying desperately to avoid it. It had been strongly suggested that I take a year off from men while I was getting sober and to my dismay he made sure I did, at least as far as he was concerned.

When my dad left for Honduras to help build houses after Hurricane Mitch I wanted to go too, but my life was still barely glued back together and traveling to a third-world country was too likely to tear it back apart. Stan went, though, just after my father, leaving on New Year's Eve of the new millennium and I wished I was strong enough to build things too.

He finally called the day after my first past life regression. "Girl, you've got a man coming into your life," the practitioner, Joan, said the moment she opened the door and saw me standing on her stoop. In my past life I was a temple priestess about to be slaughtered by a Sun God, beautiful, cold, and terrifying. Joan waved her arms over me and prayed as I relayed the images in my head. Greek sandals covering my dusty feet, huge solid gray stones of the temple walls, the betrayal of the deity, the God, the man I worshiped about to sacrifice me, to leave me for dead.

At the end of the session Joan said I had some issues with men but she had done what she could to take care of them. Stan left a message on my answering machine the next night. "I haven't seen you in a month of Sundays," he said and when I called him back he asked me out on a date. We went to a Greek restaurant in the strip mall near my house and over grape leaves and Kalamata olives the thought came to me, "this is the man I'm going to marry." We went to game night at a friend's house after and the moment we left, our friends called it, too. "Those two are getting married," they said.

"What if I'm too crazy for you?" I asked as he got to know me and I got to know him, layer by layer, inch by inch. "Water seeks its own level," he said and he held my hand and listened to every word I said.

We got married one year later to the day under the chupah my dad made out of wood from his land. My mom made the ketubah and a friend made me a gown fit for a princess. All of my bridesmaids went barefoot in different shades of lavender and purple dress.

After the ceremony that Joan officiated, Stan and I climbed into a canoe and sailed to his waiting car on the other shore. I gave all of my bridesmaids past-life regressions with Joan as my bridal gift. Our honeymoon was on Chincoteague Island, where my dad had two of his. Stan moved into the house I grew up in and we've been there ever since.

GET BORING, GIRL

On the phone with my writing mentor, Phyllis Theroux, I tried to explain how much I wanted to write my book but live wild, too. I wanted to divorce my husband and move out. Somewhere better, anywhere different. Have affairs, travel. You know. The stuff writers do.

Instead of signing off on my plan to live a more adventurous life, Phyllis Theroux quoted Flaubert. "Be regular and orderly in your life, so that you may be violent and original in your work."

"Get boring, girl," she said.

And though I still wanted to throw a grenade into my life rather than rebuild it, I never forgot what she said. It removed the poison from the itch, the burn to shake everything up and toss it all out. I thought you had to live in a castle or a ditch or at least an apartment in New York City to write. I didn't know it could be a small house in the suburbs, the house you'd grown up in, and then returned to, the same house where you were actually learning to pay your bills and maintain your relationships and stay sober, rather than burn everything to the ground.

I didn't know that staying, being responsible, and finding order could help build a nest for all of the stories flying around my life to land, to be nurtured, to hatch and to grow.

YOU ARE WRONG

Frequently during the closing circle of the classes I teach, someone shares that their writing wasn't as good as it could have been (sucked, failed, missed the point) and that they felt bad (nervous, weird, off the mark, had no idea what they were doing or why) the whole time they were writing it.

"You are wrong," I say back.

This might be harsh and surprising feedback from a writing teacher whose job is to support, encourage, and inspire. But the truth is my students are usually wrong about the quality of their writing no matter how strongly they feel. Inevitably the class loved the piece they read. And inevitably it felt like shit to write. But that's not the point. The point is that they did it anyway. And it's more beautiful than they may ever know. My students are wrong. I am wrong. And I bet you're wrong too. I have found being wrong one of the most hopeful revelations of my life.

I started to glimpse how wrong I was a few years back when I requested my college transcripts. For well over a decade I'd been haunted by the squandered waste of my higher education. My artsy independent school only gave out evaluations so I had never seen an actual grade. A friend suggested I end the misery and face the truth. When that transcript arrived my heart was in my throat. But instead of Ds and Fs, staring back at me were a lot of As with a sprinkle of Bs. I had been wrong and there was actual empirical evidence to prove it. How exciting!

Had I been wrong about anything else? I'd been sure I'd been an outcast loser in middle school. A quick hunt through the attic revealed yearbooks crammed with notes of love and affection. Maybe I'd been wrong there, too. My mind and social standing were in better shape than I'd thought but what of my monstrous body and hideous face? Go ahead and track down your old photos. Have you ever found a picture of yourself when you weren't thinner and more beautiful than you remember being at the time? I haven't.

The good news is that I believe, overall, we're wrong. At any given time we just don't know who we are or how we're doing.

I try to remember this on the days I feel my brain and life and face are cobbled together like the Bride of Frankenstein or when I'm writing something I feel particularly bad about. And I try to remind you, too.

Disclaimer: Okay, so we're probably right about a few things too, but it's gotta be a very small percentage of the time. Like, no more than 50%.

GO AWAY

One of the things I like most about writing 10 minutes at a time is that you don't have to go anywhere special to do it. You don't have to have a week at an Italian villa or a weekend at a writing retreat or even a whole hour in a coffee shop. You can write for 10 minutes in the carpool line or while the coffee's brewing, during commercial breaks or intermissions, when you get up in the morning or in your bed at night, even if someone is snoring loudly beside you.

Still, it can be really valuable to get away, to create sacred space you and your writing can coinhabit for an extended length of time. When we create a writing getaway momentum can build and we can allow the stuff that's deeper down, further hidden, the time and space to rise all the way up.

We don't have to be millionaires or childless bachelors, either. Several years ago when money was tight and my son was small, I booked a night at a motel 2.1 miles from my house with a $50 Visa gift card I'd received for Hanukkah. A writer friend and I spent 18 glorious hours writing, ordering Chinese takeout and making coffee in the bathroom. When I left at 11 a.m. checkout (after an intimate visit with the waffle bar) I felt like I'd had a short stay in Tahiti — AND I'd gotten through a snarled piece of writing too tangled to unwind in a few stolen minutes.

I've been to and led some amazing writing retreats in quaint farmhouses in the beautiful mountains of Virginia, but writing retreats can also happen in attics or basements, backyard patios, campgrounds or the local coffee shop.

Listen to your writing self. When she wants to get away, try to take her.

WRITING THE COPY

Go into your life like a reporter. Notice the details of the chores you perform during a mundane day, of your dysfunctional family, what it feels like when someone else washes your hair, your divorce, your move, your hospital stay.

Listen for dialogue, look for plot, jot down details and observations. Going into our lives like writers on the prowl for story, character, and setting helps us notice more and remember more, while creating an invisible film of distance between ourselves and the bizarre or scary or life-changing situations we find ourselves in.

This is not to take you out of your life but to plant you more firmly in it, while opening up space for a new perspective running concurrently with the old.

Many spiritual traditions encourage us to pause and respond rather than to react. When we go into our lives as writers we are more able to stand back an inch from our own internal dialogue and the people around us. We are able to consider the scene unfolding before us for an extra second in a more thoughtful, intentional way.

Every year around the holidays, I encourage my students to go into their family celebrations as reporters or to add the role of writer to whatever roles they already play in whatever they are returning to.

Our families, our neighbors and friends, the people on the street, the conversations we overhear in restaurants make great material for us to gather from the stuff of our daily lives.

Nora Ephron says that "everything is copy." This does not mean we have to expose or publish every crazy thing our family does, but we can certainly write our way through the living of it.

OVER OUR HEADS

Two weeks ago I was in deep anguish about the state of my living room...
until I saw a play about the Holocaust. The play, adapted by a local playwright
based on a book by a local author based on a true story, was gut-wrenching
and, as one may suspect, did not end happily. We're so unbelievably lucky,
I thought as the curtain fell. Maybe my living room isn't that bad after all!

And then last week I was in deep anguish once again...this time over the state
of Valentine's Day. It just wasn't unfolding quite the way I thought it should.
Until I went to hear a former Jehovah's Witness talk about recovering from
crack in the projects. My Valentine's Day was not so bad after that. And even
better when I found out my husband likes to celebrate Valentine's Day a vague
number of weeks before and the day after.

"The Holocaust, drug addiction, and systemic poverty have really brightened
my spirits the last couple of weeks!" I found myself thinking. Followed quickly
by I MUST BE THE WORST HUMAN WHO HAS EVER LIVED.

While I am both grateful and embarrassed by my need for such radical
perspective shifts, over the course of our lives I do think we take turns giving
them to each other. There have been at least a few occasions when the state
of this Jewish love-junkie alcoholic's affairs have made someone else grateful
as hell for theirs. A friend of mine who teaches mindfulness tells me that when
we complain about our high-class, first-world problems it's like complaining
about leaves in the pool. We get so focused on small inconveniences we forget
that we have POOLS. Even if they're pools we've rented or borrowed from
someone else.

And yet. Sometimes our first-world, high-class, leaves-in-the-pool problems
can trigger very real, very deep, primal pain. In just about every single writing
class I teach someone apologizes for the trivial nature of their suffering.
I know other people have it worse, they are quick to explain. Yes and no,
I think. Because when we are experiencing self-loathing, when we feel unloved
or unlovable, when we are feeling broken, it can in fact feel like drowning.

Sometimes we berate ourselves for complaining about leaves in our pool when we are way over our heads in the deep end. Sometimes I'm flailing around face first in a shallow puddle. Sometimes the leaves clog the drainage pipes and nothing new can get in or out. Listening to other people's stories and experiences and sharing the truth of my own without judgment can bring about a miraculous shift in perspective. And getting a couple of heart-shaped boxes of chocolate the day after Valentine's Day from the man I was about to sell on eBay can too.

VULTURES TO CARRION

I have never been a fan of criticism. Even constructive criticism. As an alcoholic with a rebellious personality, please don't tell me what to do. And unless I've asked, please don't tell me what I've done wrong and what I should do better. IT WILL NOT HELP. For me, criticism is barbed, burns, and so far has not once succeeded in encouraging me to find my best self and do better work.

Critique groups or the traditional workshop settings are a perfect fit for some people. Some people like to receive criticism as much as they like to dish it out. But in my mind's eye, I always picture vultures circling carrion, greedily devouring guts and entrails from a manuscript bleeding out in the center of the table. No, thank you.

In class, I ask students not to comment on each other's work for the sake of time and safety. I believe a room full of people compassionately and non-judgmentally listening to each other's stories is a far more effective way to hear and understand your own voice and the story you're trying to tell than everyone else telling you what to say and how to say it.

Giving and receiving feedback is another story. Writers crave feedback, and need it. It's part of our conversation with the world that helps our writing thrive and grow. Feedback and critiques are very different. When I give positive, strength-based feedback, I trust that what's working in a piece will rise to the surface while what isn't working as well will settle to the bottom and be sifted away like sand through a sieve. The more beautiful and buoyant parts of a piece float to the top and can be harvested in their most beautiful, natural state.

I've been accused of being too generous with my feedback as if what I say might be insincere. But the truth is, I can always find at least one thing to love or admire within a piece of writing, just as I can find at least one thing to love or admire about the person writing it.

I've seen writing wither under criticism and flourish with the lightest touch of loving guidance. Leave the carrion to the vultures. They need it more than us.

TAKE IT ALL OUT

My feet soak in sudsy hot water before the woman removes them from the tub one at a time, placing them on her bent knee and deftly sawing off the dead skin from the heel with her file. I try to relax into her chair, into her hands, into the bath at my feet but so much dead skin sloughing away makes me uneasy. Where does it go and how will I ever replace it?

The woman pampers my head after my feet, moving me this way and that, massaging my shoulders and cutting my hair. I should feel spoiled and loved but I feel floppy and numb, not exactly outside of my body but definitely not in it either.

I am driving home after this appointment, this attempt at self-care, a gift from a friend meant to somehow offset the baby that has died in my belly and lies there still, when a car flies out of nowhere and T-bones me at the intersection of Monument and Hamilton. My car spins in a circle so fast that when I stop I no longer know where I am. I walk to a curb with grass and sit down, my head spinning, my knee fat. When I call my husband to tell him what happened I tell him the wrong crossroads completely.

It is Cinco De Mayo and the girl driving the other car is drunk. I don't want to look at her. She looks just like me ten years ago, hysterical, shiny with tears. Her boyfriend tries to convince me to tell the cops he was driving instead.

An ambulance comes and I'm strapped tightly to a stretcher. I don't have to worry about being strapped too tightly, I think, because the baby is already dead. At the hospital they prescribe painkillers I need for my knee but want for my head. I don't want to feel any of this. I am sent home with plans to return three days later for surgery, surgery I now want more desperately than anything.

"Take it out. Take it all out," I beg. The same doctor who delivered my son removes my uterus. A coffin already, and also perhaps the most heroic, valiant part of me there's ever been. In the midst of so much pain and so much death and so much blood, my uterus gave me a son.

Recovery feels painless compared to the pain I've already felt. The emptiness, a lightness, a welcome relief. I will never go through any of this again.

My old car has been totaled in the crash and when it is time to buy a new car, I don't pick out another wagon. I choose an adorable, bright orange VW Bug instead. It is just big enough for our family exactly the size it already is.

STITCH YOUR STORY TOGETHER

When we first show up in a writing class, the stories from our lives might feel like shattered glass. There are fragments of memory, shards of dialogue, shadows of faces, and long forgotten enemies and friends. We have no idea how or if we'll ever be able to piece the whole thing back together again.

If we begin with even the tiniest sliver, fragment, or word and keep going, in time, the gluing and patching and stitching together of all the disparate pieces will start to take shape, forming a new pattern of its own.

Each of us has threads that wind through our lives, threads that we can follow with the pen as our needle. Our recurring thread might be food or money, sex or moving, ex-wives or husbands, addictions, gods, loss, death, or special artifacts that resurface again and again.

For some of us our theme is a person — the father we've always been seeking or the mother who appears as a ghost in our dreams. We might follow the thread of the rooms in our house or our own children born, grown, or dead. We might recount the rings on our fingers or the countries where we've been.

I've written out my waitressing history, haircuts, bad boyfriends, brands of alcohol, and cars I've driven. What images or themes continue to appear in your life again and again?

You don't have to know what your defining thread will be when you begin. Keep allowing the fragments of memory and time and feelings to come. At the end, your story might have a very different shape than the story you thought would come, but it will be yours, unearthed and pieced back together again.

THE NON-WRITING WRITER

"A non-writing writer is a monster courting insanity," writes Franz Kafka.

My life is right when I write, I like to say. For me writing is like bathing. I don't do it every day, but if too many days go by I start to notice.

I meet many people who used to love to write but have gone months, years, decades without writing. Jobs, marriages, school, children, vacation, dishes, laundry, Christmas, taxes, all got in the way. I believe it's never too late, we've never gone too far to come back whether after two days or 20+ years. The writer inside of us still wants and needs to come out. Sometimes that writer must be coaxed, but sweetly, gently, not with punishment or whips or chains.

I've lost track of a regular writing practice during numerous periods of my life. On the dude ranch in Colorado, the farm in Arkansas, between miscarriages when I worked at the preschool. I've made a practice, not of writing every single day, but of allowing myself to return to writing after I've been away.

If I sit back down with the goal to write something I can publish I'm doomed before I even begin. But if I sit down to write as a way of returning to myself, to find out who has been inside all this time and what they have been wanting to tell me, then the page welcomes me home with warm open arms every single time.

CHAPTER 10

Miraculous Birth

BIRTHS AND BOOKS

My son was born in the midst of a maelstrom of miscarriages, before three and after three, via emergency C-section with the cord triple-wrapped around his neck. I was terrified that every day of this pregnancy would be the last. I'd wanted a natural childbirth at home but the midwife said I was far too high-risk. It was hard to surrender the dream of the way I wanted to give birth but the fact that my son was born at all was a miracle itself. The fact that he's brilliant and handsome is just icing on the cake. I wailed and grieved and mourned the losses of the babies I didn't have, but the one I did have is everything to me now. How he got here no longer matters at all.

As I write the book that contains my blood and heart and soul it occurs to me that how it comes into the world is of less consequence than whether or not it does. If I want to mother this story it doesn't matter if it's published by Random House or Kinko's, if a million people read it or one. I was a mother even to the babies I didn't have.

We can study the ins and outs of the publishing industry but that's no guarantee of publication. It's hard to hear parenting advice when you have no idea whether or not you'll be able to have a baby. I have authored manuscripts that will never be published. I hope with all of my heart that the book I'm writing now has a smooth, beautiful, easy birth, but no matter what, I still get to love it. I still get to claim it as mine.

CRAFT

After I get married, I throw myself into scrapbooking, hard. I become a scrapbooking consultant. I have coffins of unsorted photographs that call to me like the undead. Specialty scrapbooking stores are popping up all over town. Only they don't really have the accessories I need most to make my photo collages complete.

Where are the stickers featuring spilled bottles of wine and crumpled packs of cigarettes? Where are the "I blacked out for this part" foam cut-outs or the backgrounds that make everything just a little off-kilter and blurry? How do you photo-document miscarriage or grief? How do I narrate addiction, heartbreak, or recovery with bright paper cut-outs?

Still my need to crop, organize, and arrange the past in a linear way that makes some kind of sense to me is strong. I go to classes and workshops and conventions. I set up scrapbooking parties. I scrapbook the hell out of our wedding and college and high school and Italy and Eastern Europe, Colorado and Arkansas and Alaska and childhood as best I can but nothing fits as tidily between the plastic sheet protectors in the huge bright albums as succinctly as I'd like.

Because I buy so many scrapbooking supplies, my scrapbooking business does not make one dollar. So I quit and throw myself into stained glass making instead. I get a job at a stained glass shop in the East End, cutting glass and skin, trying not to bleed onto the frames and mirrors. I drag home boxes of shiny colored bits of broken glass. I solder magic wands and whimsical wall hangings and business card holders, most of which collapse in on themselves after a week or two.

So, I take up crochet, and crochet miles and miles of lumpy, scratchy scarves that I give away, that I never wear.

I craft madly to avoid the thing I want to do most: write everything down.

Until at last, at last, I do. I start to write everything down.

LIBRARIES INSIDE ME

When I was 15, my best friend Sarah and I flew to Seattle to help my mother sell inspirational buttons at an AA convention.

Sarah was intellectual and sharp, bewitching and blossoming, a real beauty. We'd been best friends since we were five, but now that we were teenagers, I kept an unspoken score card in my head, one where she was always winning. All the boys loved her. She'd already traveled to various countries around the world. She'd engage in philosophical and political debates that I didn't even know how to enter. I was in love with her and jealous of her. I knew she had something I could never have, was someone I could never be. We were standing on a street corner in Seattle, waiting to cross, talking about our lives and our dreams, our pasts and our futures, when she told me she felt like she had libraries inside her.

Oh shit, I thought. I might only have a pamphlet. I couldn't imagine how my experiences or dreams or memories or thoughts could ever fill a book, much less the vastness of an entire library.

Thirty-seven years later, Sarah and I are still friends. And while I adore her, her degrees, her international travels, her experiences in exotic countries, I like my own libraries now too, the books I'm filling inside of them. Less and less do I feel the need to compare us to each other. Her stories are hers, hard won, and so are mine. We have a friendship that has survived decades and marriages and falling outs and deep hurts but ridiculous amounts of love and laughter and intimacy and sharing, too. Our libraries are intact and they keep growing. The beauty of her stories does not diminish the beauty of mine.

OOPS! I ACCIDENTALLY SELF-PUBLISHED MY FIRST BOOK

I really really like your book, and not just because I'm your mother.
— My mother

One January a few years ago, a psychic named Reverend Dave told me I was going to self-publish my first book. I would have laughed in his face if we hadn't been on the phone. The hell I am! There was no way he was right about this even though he was right about a lot of other things. Suddenly I hated him.

Brought up in the hardcore world of literary arts, my plan was and always had been to find an agent who would then find a small but respectable publishing house so help me God if it was the last thing I ever did.

But then, the prototype for *The Halfway House for Writers* came in the mail. In the beginning of that year when I'd been asked to teach a master class that fall, I realized it was time to create original source material for my classes. I had two great writers and friends, Sarah Allen-Short and Anne Carle Carson, help me organize my thoughts. I had the amazing Bird Cox help me with layout. I chose a gorgeous drawing by artist Mary Chiaramonte for the cover. But despite my intention to make a really lovely downloadable PDF or a zine or a pile of papers stapled together at Kinko's, my talented friend, editor, and graphic designer, Rob Collins, made the pages I wrote look an awful lot like a book.

Son of a bitch! I thought when a single copy of that book arrived in the mail. Reverend Dave was right! And I cried for an hour. Sobbed. I couldn't figure out all of the feelings immediately but then they came clear. If I was going to self-publish my first book it had goddamn well better be good. And all of the missing sections, the chapters I hadn't written or had left out, formed like connective tissue in my brain.

I started writing furiously, staying up late, waking up early, uncovering half-finished works and getting other pieces ready. Luckily, the very next day I happened to be on my way to a retreat previously dedicated to my longer manuscript, but completing *The Halfway House for Writers* took all priority. It came and came and came until Sunday morning it was done.

"I'm done," I said. "I've written a book," I said. "A book I'm going to publish myself." And I felt happy. Sema Wray, a beloved writing student on that retreat who'd given me a tiara for my 40th birthday, offered to throw me a launch party. I said, "Yes, please!" I asked Ward Tefft if he'd be willing to sell my book at Chop Suey Books and he said, "Are you kidding? Of course!" I asked my mother, a former English teacher, to read the second prototype that came in the mail and even though she's my mother the fact that she loved it made my heart soar. In fact, I think I should blurb her on the back.

Reverend Dave was right. After all, my entire handbook is about healing from our writing wounds, finding the joy in creation, telling the truth and letting the process unfold naturally so I guess it makes perfect sense that, even unintentionally, I ended up proving my own point. I felt I knew best about the direction my writing life should go but I had been dead wrong.

WRITING BABY

Right now Henry is at home deciding if he wants to be a professor, a politician, or a journalist with his own media conglomerate. He's already interviewed a delegate and a senator, written for the ACLU of Virginia blog and *RVA Magazine*. He's started a civil rights club and hosted fundraisers for causes he believes in. He's also currently writing a book. Every time I turn around, he's doing something else I find nearly impossible to believe.

When he was born I called him my Writing Baby. I returned to a fiction class at the museum pregnant with him after so many years away, got the job as Book Editor the week he was born, wrote articles and conducted interviews while he nursed at my breast. Those long afternoons reading books for review while he napped beside me on our king-sized bed. Last night he said, "I thought my first job would be at McDonald's," but now he's a 13-year-old activist and has a paid column instead.

When I was 13, I wrote an essay for a local teen magazine about how I would break the cycle of addiction in my family. The next year I had my first drink and embarked on a sage career of drugs and alcoholism instead.

A writer in my Tuesday morning class said someone forgot to tell Henry that the stuff he's doing is hard and yes, I marvel at his confidence. The phone calls he makes and the emails he sends like a person with agency and security and the ability to follow through and get things done. I'm in awe of his kindness, his humor, his face, the parts of his father and me that came together to create something not of us, but of itself, complete.

Last night I lay in bed reading an article about a cross-eyed woman who was arrested for training her squirrels to attack her boyfriend (they severed both an ear and a testicle) while Henry wrote both his first column for *RVA Magazine* about yesterday's school walkout and a position paper on the Yemen crisis for the Model UN. He came in every few minutes to read me this or ask me that and the more intense his arguments and sentences became, the more fiercely I searched for dumb things to look at on the Internet. Who is this kid?

When he packed for his three-day trip to Virginia Beach for the student government convention, he carefully laid out his items of clothing in the reverse order he would need to wear them.

"Look!" I say. "The form says you can bring drinks and snacks!"

"No thanks, Mom," he says politely and then I wonder who the hell he is.

I was sad to see that he'd packed up all of his NASA posters and most of his model rockets to give away or auction off on eBay, that part of his life now folded into the others: magician, mailman, bowling alley repair person.

I ask him if he wants to continue his column after his trial term is up and he says, "Probably, but I'll have to raise my rates." Right now he's paying another kid five bucks to input the edits he made on his book manuscript. No more wrapping him up in a towel when he gets out of the bath calling to Stan, "Hey! I have a present for you!" and after the handoff Stan saying, "It's just what I've always wanted!" No more hiding under the covers pretending to be invisible while Stan searches for us all over the house, before rolling over us on the bed.

When he was born three weeks early with positional clubfeet, squashed into my irregularly-shaped uterus, when he had to be hospitalized for a week with RSV and walking pneumonia at two months old on IVS in an incubator, when he had to have hypospadias surgery at 18 months, after all those heart-wrenching losses already, I said, "God you owe me." I think God listened.

WRITING EVERYONE CAN UNDERSTAND

Since *The Halfway House for Writers* was published, I have led a workshop, spoken, or given a reading for entrepreneurs and creatives, yogis in teacher training, county school librarians, women in recovery, women in a correctional facility, university students, medical students, copywriters, and a few people who showed up for a book discussion in a gas station garage. Each experience has been beautiful, terrifying, humbling, and life-giving, resonating with the feeling that I was exactly where I was supposed to be.

The thing is, I never saw myself doing any of these things. Not in a million years.

Once upon a time I wanted to grow up to be a literary novelist who wrote High Art for literary readers. In college I was embarrassed when my girlfriend said I wrote stories anyone could understand. There was no subterfuge. I hadn't planted any clues. Her poetry was beautiful and cryptic. I wished I could copy it. I wanted to write something that would leave the academics and critics scratching their heads while begging for more. But that wasn't the plan for me.

I never planned to start a summer camp for kids. I never planned to self-publish my first book. In fact, when I realized I had self-published my first book I cried my eyes out. I never wanted to look people in the eye while using words like *hope* and *love* and *nourish* and *inspire*. I wanted to be cooler and edgier than that. I wanted to give readings in crowded, dark, smoky cafés. I wanted to crawl home from seedy bars in big cities at 3 a.m. and write about everything I didn't remember the next morning. I wanted to get married and divorced a minimum of three times so I could write about that too. At the very least I wanted to go to an expensive graduate school so I could slum around with the other broke writers and drink and smoke and look damn hip and tragic while doing it.

But none of those things happened. In fact, pretty much everything I've ever tried to make happen hasn't. But everything I've stepped out of the way for has. In fact, lately I have been so overwhelmed by the possibilities, so excited by the potential and people and stories peering and poking out from every nook and cranny I look behind these days I can barely sit still.

Turns out, I didn't have to plant any clues, I just had to keep my eyes open for the ones that hit me over the head.

I no longer want to read only the writing of the elite, well-published, pedigreed few. I want to read writers who don't even know they are writers, people without a particular position or pedigree but rich with experience and yes, hope and inspiration and love, no matter how far down they've been or where they've come from or what they call themselves now.

I want to read writing everyone can understand.

THE PEOPLE WHO WRITE WITH ME

I want to tell you about the people who write with me. After you give them the once-over, the first glance, the up-and-down, you might think that one's really got her shit together but boy is he falling apart. You might think white black brown gay straight rich poor, you might succumb to a stereotype before you have the chance to think twice. But when my students start to share the heart, blood, mind, soul, guts, love, life, memory, and story they've laid across the page, translating rage and love and loss into pen and ink, paper and pencil you will know them in a way you might only know yourself. A way that connects eye to eye, heart to heart, past all the trappings and assumptions that keep us stuck, frozen on the outside, in our differences and separation.

I fall in love with each of my students as they create sacred circles around square tables. In showing me themselves, they show me to me. They expand my world, feeding me stories more nourishing than food, more heartbreaking than breakups, more funny than stand up, more real than sometimes life in the living of it.

They are brave, they are deep, they are audacious. They are accomplished writers and storytellers and they are introverted recluses who rarely leave the house, have never read in front of a group. They are brilliant, they are raw, they are real. And they are here tonight.

I usually feel so selfish and greedy, gobbling up their talent and hoarding it all for myself. So it is a real joy and a pleasure to get to share some of them with you.

Here they are.

Beautiful.

Beautiful.

Beautiful.

MIRACULOUS BIRTH

Breasts

My breasts are planets, stars, meteors, heavenly bodies. They are wrecking balls, bulldogs, fully-inflated birthday balloons. My nipples had no feeling until I gave birth to my son, and with all that sucking and mewing and grappling he gave them the life that they in turn gave him. My breasts defy Victoria's Secret, beg for an engineer, need structural and architectural support, blueprints, infrastructure, hard bites, and kisses.

In high school a friend and I turned the lights off and weighed our breasts on her mother's bathroom scale. Naturally her mother walked in, turned the lights on, asked if we were lesbians. Were we? It was not an either/or question, as I would later discover. Then, we were scientists in search of evidence, detectives in search of a clue.

Skin

My mother told me that if you connected my birthmarks from head to toe you'd get a map of the constellations, and that the big one between the small of my back and tailbone was where the angels kissed me. Maybe that's why I have never wanted a tattoo. I was born with a map on my skin, my very own connect-the-dots.

Thighs

My thighs are strong and jiggly and burn their way up stairs and down mountains, through squats and lunges and rolling hills. They wrap around backs like bows around a present. They are liquid rumbling. Would a volcano apologize? Would an earthquake promise to occupy less space?

Right Hip

Every story I haven't written or am currently afraid to write is compressed into my right hip. The massage therapist presses her thumb into the acute horror of my life and it vanishes without being adequately expressed, right there in that hinge in the center of me. I'd been told I had child-bearing hips, but I didn't know they would bear so many of my stories, too.

Feet

My father had such big feet that when he was a little boy people said he looked like the capital letter L. My mother planted seeds in her last pair of high heels, planters now for new life on her front porch. My mother and I have inverse bodies. I'm big where she's small and vice versa. It's like she cut out her own negative space and used it to make me. My father is a planet all his own.

On my wedding day, I went barefoot. Tiny splinters stabbed through the flesh between my heels and toes. On that king-sized bed in the hotel where I spent my first night newly-cleaved to the man who was now my husband, their extraction caused far more curiosity than pain.

Hands

My father told me he'd buy me a car when my hands got as big as his, and for that I am still waiting. My mother's hands were always stained with oil paint, clay, dirt; she rarely wore rings or polish.

Agreeing to wear the same platinum bands on one hand for the rest of my life was bigger than spoken vows.

My hands have kept and broken promises. Scratched and drawn blood. Blessed, prayed, and been formed into fists.

Eyes

At birth my eyes were gunmetal blue according to my mother, but my best friend in elementary school said they were the color of cement. My mother's and father's and husband's eyes are brown holes dug out of the center of the earth, while in my blue/green/gray I have often felt like a cat lost far out at sea.

Hunger

The only thing I've ever truly understood about my body was what I wanted to put inside of it. Pink wine sweeter than Kool-Aid, coils of black smoke, liquid fire, the creamy bite of strong coffee, enough food to at last feel secure, safe, sated. I don't know how hunger works but I know how I want my body to feel when I'm willing to feel it at all: like an animal that has found a home in this loose casing of skin.

Belly

A thirteen-inch scar zig-zags down the side to a cut above the pubic bone: soft pink jagged lines where the skin was cut, sewn, and stapled. Bled.

The steps up to our bed, which my husband built, the bandages he changed, the wounds he cleaned, the days and weeks in the gauzy filmy haze of the hospital, the tumors, the unborn. The parts of me removed and then sent to Pathology: a uterus, a gallbladder, an adrenal gland, a rib, all those unborn babies.

Hair

A meteorological disturbance beyond my control or command, my hair answers to no one. My husband too has unruly thick black hair, hair that precedes him into a room. Our son has blonde hair with specks of gold and red and orange and I try to decode him one strand at a time.

A Thank-You Note

"Your body is not a thank-you note," my mother wrote to me in a card when I was in Alaska, half in love with the captain of the fleet, half in love with the deaf deckhand teaching me American Sign Language. Half-dead, half-drunk, half-sober, half-crazy.

Oh, but it was. It had been. It has also been my passport, my license, my excuse, my getaway car before it became a grave, a temple, a tombstone. My body has been a deadweight lump of unformed clay that I've kneaded and rolled and tried to shape, full of hidden treasure I've been desperate to find and spend. I've thrown it at strangers, hidden it from my husband, given it like a shield of flesh, an orchard of sustenance, a playground to my son.

Invitation

Sit on my lap, feast on me. My body is not a thank-you note but it has been an invitation. Yes, I feel like Mother Earth. Yes, I feel like Eve. I want to form and grow and then eat the apple.

The body is, in parts, digestible like an apple. An elbow, a pinkie, a knee. Add the whole thing up and you have a universe lumbering around, trying to change and break and make the world with sex and death and babies.

It is a beautiful mystery to be a woman. We get the opportunity every single day to learn how to love ourselves the way we might learn to love the universe at the beginning of time. Life has started and ended in my womb and now my womb is gone and yet my body is still magic, a magician who has lost her hat but memorized her spells. I sit and walk and kneel and do normal human things, but don't all the gods, isn't that part of their charm?

My body is not a thank-you note but it is a prayer, a song, a mourner's kaddish, an announcement of miraculous birth.

MINE

You sound like a mewling tiny kitten stuck in a tree. I yell at your father to leave me on the table, numb from the neck down and cut in half, to go to you. "Go get him!" I shout. "I'm not leaving you," he says and grips my hand and I squeeze back, wanting him to stay and needing him to go, to rescue you from that teetering branch, swaying wildly, precariously in the wind, where they are saving your life with tubes crammed down your throat. This might be our last moment together, alone, ever again, but my heart is exploding with your mews that I can hear from the operating table.

"Go to him," I plead and he does, finally, your father, and they let him bring you to me swaddled tight. You suck furiously at your father's nose and you are not a kitten, but a baby boy, scrunchy and red-faced and totally determined to be alive. My heart blooms as I look at you. You open and close your tiny mouth and latch onto my nose while I scramble to uncover a real nipple, a real breast. They are sewing me shut while I feed you, this new part of myself that I've met for the first time today.

I measure ten centimeters from the arch of your nose to the top of your curved lip. There are fat, fleshy cheeks and earth-round eyes that flutter-flutter-blink. I touch both of your ears: soft sourdough pretzels, no salt. I smell your hair. It is milk and kittens and a little of my insides that you brought out for me to consider. Your face changes every second or so—a lens without a filter, a rippling puddle of kerosene illuminating the rainbows.

You have a perfectly round head that did not get molded into a point through the birth canal. The umbilical cord that sustained you inside my body wrapped itself around your neck three times, bringing you into the world with a sudden and messy explosion of life. I did not have the natural birth that terrified me as a child, but that I had painstakingly planned as a young wife.

You are an emergency bowling ball that bursts through my heart-shaped uterus. When the doctor cuts me, blood sprays across the faces of the nurses and attending doctors and I think "Is this normal?" and days later when I learn that it isn't I have a fruit and chocolate basket delivered to the office.

My whole family prays in a circle, clasping hands in the waiting room, expectant, terrified, hopeful, and bursting with love.

Life turned out not to be the stories I'd heard or the plans that I'd mapped out, but all of the parts of it, beautiful, terrible, and somehow held together, are mine.

Life in 10 Minutes Press

Surrender Your Weapons is the first book published by Life in 10 Minutes Press, a hybrid press showcasing work that is brave, beautiful, honest, raw, experimental, and vital.

At Life in 10 Minutes Press, we aim to bridge the gap between writers and publishing and promote the books we want to see in the world.

We are especially passionate about memoir by women and gender-nonconforming writers, nonfiction that challenges the status quo, and boundary-breaking books of all genres.

All books published with Life in 10 Minutes Press are carefully chosen to support our mission and reflect our commitment to promoting fresh, engaging, high-quality storytelling.

Learn more about publishing your book or donating to our scholarship fund at **www.lifein10minutes.com/press**!

acknowledgments

Thank you to the editors for publishing early excerpts of this manuscript.

"Prom Queen" was published in *Tarnished: True Stories of Innocence Lost,* edited by Shawna Kenney and Cara Bruce.

"Pilgrims to Mecca" was published in *Into Quarterly: A Creative City Journal.*

"Shit List, Wish List, Thank You List" was published on resistance365.com.

"Exotic Names of Gods and Children" was published on parhelion. com.

"The Body, In Parts" was published in *Broad Street Magazine.*

colophon

Surrender Your Weapons is set in Sabon, an old-style serif typeface designed by typographer and graphic designer Jan Tschichold.

The book was designed by Llewellyn Hensley / Content-Aware Graphic Design (content-aware.design).